VGM Opportunities Series

OPPORTUNITIES IN
CARPENTRY
CAREERS

Roger Sheldon

Foreword by
Sigurd Lucassen
Former General President
United Brotherhood of Carpenters
and Joiners of America

VGM Career Horizons
NTC/Contemporary Publishing Group

Library of Congress Cataloging-in-Publication Data

Sheldon, Roger.
    Opportunities in carpentry careers / Roger Sheldon ; foreword by
Sigurd Lucassen.
        p. cm. — (VGM opportunities series)
      ISBN 0-8442-3408-7 (cloth). — ISBN 0-8442-3424-9 (pbk.)
      1. Carpentry—Vocational guidance. I. Title. II. Series.
TH5608.8.S54   1999
694'.023—dc21
                                        99–34063
                                              CIP

Cover photographs: © PhotoDisc, Inc.

Published by VGM Career Horizons
A division of NTC/Contemporary Publishing Group, Inc.
4255 West Touhy Avenue, Lincolnwood (Chicago), Illinois 60712-1975 U.S.A.
Copyright © 2000 by NTC/Contemporary Publishing Group, Inc.
Printed in the United States of America
International Standard Book Number: 0-8442-3408-7 (cloth)
                                       0-8442-3424-9 (paper)
99 00 01 02 03 04 LB 18 17 16 15 14 13 12 11 10 9 8 7 6 5 4 3 2

CONTENTS

About the Author vii

Foreword ix

Preface xi

1. One of Mankind's Oldest Trades 1

Origin of the term *carpenter*. Largest group of skilled craftspeople. The timeless need of carpenters. Wood: the basic building material. Today's carpenter. Future outlook.

2. All in a Day's Work 9

Who is boss on the job? Days without work. Specialty workdays.

3. The Carpenter in the 21st Century 15

New techniques and tools. Housing and city planning. To the ocean's depths. More giant steps in space?

4. Is Carpentry for You? 19

Profile of a carpenter. Carpentry training and education. The future belongs to men and women of skill. What to expect in financial returns. What authorities say. The status of the carpenter.

5. Preparing for a Carpentry Career 29

High school preparation. Trade schools. Pre-apprenticeship. Work as a carpenter's helper. Why apprenticeship?

 6. **Choosing a Specialty** 35

The general carpenter. The cabinetmaker. The millwright.
The resilient floor layer. The pile driver. The shipwright.
Other occupations.

 7. **The Advantages and Disadvantages of a Career
    in Carpentry** 43

Seasonality. On-the-job hazards. Health and welfare.
Casual work opportunities. Union or nonunion.

 8. **How to Get Started** 49

Making applications. Entering the program. Term of
apprenticeship. On-the-job training. Required work
experience. Work experience for other specialties. Work
experience: related trade skills. Related school instruction.
Carpentry training in Canada. The Performance Evaluated
Training System.

 9. **What to Expect During Training** 69

Wages and working conditions. On-the-job safety.
Governed by national standards.

10. **Special Avenues to Carpentry** 75

The Job Corps. Training for Native Americans. The
Vocational Industrial Clubs of America. Training
in Canada. Other avenues to carpentry.

11. **Professional Organizations** 85

Early craft guilds. Management organizations.

12. **Related Fields and Broader Horizons** 91

Other areas of advancement. Working for yourself.

Appendix A: Glossary 95

Appendix B: Related Publications 105

Appendix C: State and Territorial Apprenticeship Councils/Agencies **109**

Appendix D: Regional Offices, U.S. Bureau of Apprenticeship and Training **115**

Appendix E: State Offices, U.S. Bureau of Apprenticeship and Training **119**

Appendix F: Accredited Trade Schools **129**

Appendix G: Trade Associations. **147**

ABOUT THE AUTHOR

Roger Sheldon was, before his retirement, communications director of the United Brotherhood of Carpenters and Joiners of America. He was managing editor of the organization's magazine, *The Carpenter,* and served as an editorial consultant to the publication before becoming associate editor in 1973. He has served as an editorial advisor to several labor organizations and has done special work for the United States Department of Labor. In 1962 he served as information officer for President John Kennedy's Commission on the Status of Women under Eleanor Roosevelt.

For more than a decade, Mr. Sheldon was vice-president and editorial director of Merkle Press, Inc., of Washington, DC.

A native of Baton Rouge, Louisiana, and a graduate in journalism from Louisiana State University, Mr. Sheldon was an information officer with the War Assets Administration and public relations counsel to several organizations before moving to the nation's capital in 1951.

FOREWORD

Each generation of North Americans must build and rebuild many of our cities, airports, harbors, schools, retail stores, streets, highways and bridges, industrial plants. The sound of hammers, power saws, and other tools can be heard above the din of construction.

It's the sound of skilled carpenters of many specialties creating the world of the future. Carpenters are the master builders, working in a trade that goes back to the beginning of civilization.

Their craft will be performing its skilled workmanship generation after generation. There will be new tools, new building materials, and new techniques of construction. These developments will not replace the basic skills of carpentry, handed down from journeyman to apprentice, year after year, as it has been for centuries.

If you like to work with tools and with wood and other building materials to create structures of lasting value, I would suggest to you the trade of carpentry. The construction projects of tomorrow can be in your hands, and in the hands of thousands like you, in a highly respected and gratifying trade.

Sigurd Lucassen
Former General President
United Brotherhood of Carpenters
and Joiners of America

PREFACE

Carpentry is one of humanity's oldest trades. You can build a lifetime career in it the same way an experienced carpenter builds a structure—by carefully analyzing your building site, studying and understanding blueprints and specifications, collecting your tools and building materials—in other words, fully preparing yourself for the task before you.

Or you can drift aimlessly into the fringes of the trade by assuming that all a carpenter has to know to "make a living" is how to hammer a nail, saw a piece of lumber, and look through the classified advertisements for "carpenter wanted" notices.

This book is not for the drifter who chooses that latter course. Instead, it's prepared to show how you can become a truly skilled craftsperson, proud of your ability, and capable of earning a lifetime income in a basic and expanding industry.

For the young person who wants to build, create, and work as a vital part of a building and construction team, there is no more gratifying profession than that of carpentry.

We commend to you the virtues—in fact, the necessity—of apprenticeship training. There is no substitute for classroom study and on-the-job training in the field of carpentry.

Many of America's achievements in the years ahead are going to be borne in the hands of the carpentry apprentices of today. Many who read this manual and take their first steps into carpentry will share in this promising future.

CHAPTER 1

ONE OF MANKIND'S OLDEST TRADES

All across the United States and Canada today, skilled carpenters are measuring, sawing, leveling, and nailing wood in pursuit of their proud and ancient craft. They are installing tile and insulation board and placing composition shingles and aluminum siding. They are working with many new tools and materials to erect skyscrapers, build new homes, and construct bridges, boats, tunnels, and highways. Wherever people build, carpenters will be found.

ORIGIN OF THE TERM *CARPENTER*

It was the Romans who gave carpenters their name. In so-called "low" Latin, the word for wagon maker or chariot maker is *carpentarius.*

The chariot makers who followed the Roman legions were skilled woodworkers. They were employed to build housing for the armies wherever they spent the winter or established a post.

When the Romans were among the Franks, these Germanic people watched the *carpentarius* framing bridges, repairing wagons, and building barracks. In ancient French, the Roman word was changed to *charpentier,* and when this word passed into the Anglo-Saxon tongue it became, eventually, *carpenter.*

LARGEST GROUP OF SKILLED CRAFTSPEOPLE

Carpenters make up the largest single group of skilled workers in the United States today. According to the U.S. Bureau of Labor Statistics, in 1996 they held some 996,000 jobs. They will continue to play a vital role in North America and around the world as nations develop and the populations grow.

The carpenter has been a highly respected artisan since the dawn of civilization. With crude stone axes, early peoples built huts and enclosures to protect themselves from the weather and from enemies. Those individuals who excelled in the use of these ancient tools were highly respected members of society.

One of the earliest references to carpenters was in the story of Noah, who, according to Biblical legend, built an ark 300 cubits (about 450 feet) long to house two of each living thing.

Skilled carpenters sawed the cedars of Lebanon and erected Solomon's Temple. Skilled carpenters also helped build the classic temples of ancient Greece. These Greek builders used ingenious wood-construction methods to create some of the many wonders of the ancient world.

Carpenters helped the Romans spread their civilization to the frontiers of Gaul and early Britain.

THE TIMELESS NEED OF CARPENTERS

The first European colonists in America realized an immediate need for individuals skilled in the trades. Standing on the north shore of the James River, Captain John Smith of the Virginia Company looked about him and saw people from the English court with gilded laces on their clothing and fancy buckles on their shoes. Soldiers and adventurers abounded, but he found few men and women who were skilled with their hands and trained to fell trees, build stockades, whittle pegs, drive nails, mold candles, repair clothing, and perform the countless other tasks that spelled survival in the wilderness.

He wrote to Sir Walter Raleigh in protest: "When you send again, I entreat you to rather send but thirty carpenters, husbandmen, gardeners, fishermen, masons, and diggers of trees' roots, well provided, than a thousand such as we have."

The Pilgrims who settled in New England also realized the value of carpentry skills. There were more carpenters on the Mayflower than persons skilled in any other craft.

As the young United States pushed westward, carpenters erected its new towns, helped build its railroads and bridges, and joined in building the ships that made the new nation the master of the seas.

Carpentry is truly a career that grows with America. As more and more Americans move from farms and small towns into big cities, the need for new housing, new industries, and new public facilities will require the skills of the carpenter and other construction workers.

Carpenters create an amazing variety of things. A century ago, carpenters sometimes spent their idle winter months building carousels and toys for youngsters. Almost two thousand of them helped construct Walt Disney World in Florida, and more than eight hundred are regularly employed to maintain that big recreation facility. In the 1970s, they helped build the missile silos for our national defense, the Alaskan Pipeline, the big superdomes for sports events, and the spectator stands for the inaugurations of our presidents.

Carpentry has even figured in our relations with other countries. The underdeveloped nations of the world seeking Peace Corps volunteers often ask for carpenters and other persons trained in construction work, as well as teachers and other specialists. One highly valued CARE package is a kit of carpentry tools designed to be used by workers in underdeveloped countries.

WOOD: THE BASIC BUILDING MATERIAL

The basic material with which a carpenter works is wood. It has always been the primary material used in the majority of structures built in the United States. Few buildings of any kind are started without the use of wood. It is used in forms for pouring concrete, in staking out building sites, in scaffolding, in framing, and in finish work.

There are, in some cases, substitute materials (and carpenters work with these, too), but lumber and wood products still rank as the top choice for their structural performance and fine finish in housing and other light construction.

As a building material, wood has many advantages. It can be turned into many shapes without difficulty. It has great strength for its weight, and yet it has resilience, durability, and an attractive appearance.

Wood is one of the oldest building materials known to civilization, yet its versatility enables people to use it in a variety of new ways including as veneer, in laminations, and as free forms. It is even ground and mixed with other substances to be molded into tough new building materials.

Through glued lamination, lumber can be produced in many large sizes and shapes that cannot be cut freely at the lumber mill. Today, huge laminated-wood arches add grace and beauty to churches, auditoriums, and bridges where before only structural steel or reinforced concrete could be used.

New fastenings and framing devices have increased wood's adaptability in construction and multiplied the opportunities for employment in carpentry. Component building systems—building with preassembled parts instead of from rough materials—are increasing in use. In modular construction whole sections of a home or other buildings are fabricated by machines and skilled workers before being assembled into master structures.

Through conservation practices, such as tree farms and new harvesting techniques, lumber producers ensure a constant supply of wood and wood products for the future.

Research work done by the U.S. Forest Service and private industry has added considerably to the know-how of the construction industry and makes today's carpenter more versatile than ever before.

TODAY'S CARPENTER

The days when a carpenter needed only a hammer, a saw, and some nails are long past. Today's carpenters work with tiles, insulation boards, plastics, light metals, composition shingles, and acoustical materials. And these are only a fraction of the various building materials at their disposal.

The carpenter measures, saws, fits, and hammers. He or she uses levels, plumb bobs, planes, precision levels, chisels, and other hand or machine tools. The carpenter's tool chest will most likely contain hundreds of dollars worth of special-purpose tools and instruments. In addition, the carpenter's employer often supplies hundreds of dollars more in power tools and equipment.

Today's carpenter ranges from the "rough" carpenter, who erects basic frameworks, concrete forms, scaffolding, docks, and railroad trestles, to the "finish" carpenter, who must fit wood perfectly for hardwood floors, cabinets, and stairs, and attach doorknobs and other hardware.

Some carpenters do every type of carpentry work. Others tend to specialize. In rural areas, for example, the carpenter will more than likely be an all-around worker, even preparing and pouring the concrete, doing the painting, installing plate glass—being a jack-of-all trades. In the cities, however, work specialization and union jurisdictions govern much of the work. Many carpenters, for example, are employed full-time in the remodeling, repairing, and maintenance of older buildings and industrial plants. In addition, certain carpenters might install only acoustical panels. Others may specialize in trim work, while still others only hang doors or install fixtures.

A growing field of activity is the installation of interior systems. This includes the erection of movable wall partitions, the installation of metal frame ceilings with various sizes of fiberboard and tile, and the setting up of elevated flooring so that wiring, computer cables, and piping can run beneath them.

In home building carpenters begin at the foundation, helping to stake out the job; prepare the forms for concrete; and, when the foundation is set, build the structural framework—studs, joists, rafters. They put in the subflooring and sheath the roof. If they are working on a frame house, they finish the outside walls with insulation, sheathing, and siding. They may even do the final roofing. Carpenters lay the floors, hang the doors and windows, cut and fit the baseboards and other trim, and build stairs and handrails. They set door locks and other hardware and build and install cabinets and other built-in features.

The *Dictionary of Occupational Titles,* compiled by the U.S. Department of Labor, lists more than one hundred different specialties in the carpentry field. A skilled journeyman carpenter can usually perform any of these varied jobs after a brief "postgraduate" indoctrination.

FUTURE OUTLOOK

The construction industry, in which the carpenter plays a vital role, is a brawny giant. Each year projects totaling well over $86 billion (or approximately 10 percent of our gross national product) are undertaken in the United States.

In the years to come, the sounds of hammers and power saws will continue to echo in new churches, new schools, and new hospitals. The staccato of construction tools will be heard in new industrial plants and along thousands of miles of interstate expressways. Large or small, each project will be put together by men and women trained in many craft skills.

The construction industry is one of the largest in the country by dollar volume, and it is growing. According to the Associated General Contractors of America, buildings erected in the last ten years alone are equal in value to all the buildings erected since our nation was founded.

Construction requires a higher proportion of skilled workers— two out of every three—than almost any other industry. This compares with one in five in manufacturing and transportation and fewer than one in ten in other industries.

Carpentry is the leading skilled trade in the construction field, employing more than twice as many workers as are employed in the next ranking trade.

As a result, employment of carpenters is expected to increase as fast as the average of all occupations through the next century, according to the U.S. Department of Labor. It is estimated that more than seventy thousand new carpenters will be needed each year to take the place of those who retire and to fill new jobs created.

CHAPTER 2

ALL IN A DAY'S WORK

A typical workday for a carpenter begins early. Like the farmer of yesteryear, the carpenter traditionally rises before daybreak and is hard at work before the sun is hot and high in the sky. Though modern construction methods and temporary shelters from weather have eased the problems of the sun's heat and the winter's cold, carpenters and construction craftspeople continue to start work before the sun's rays bring sweat to the working people's brows.

The traditional carpenter was dressed for the job in tough, durable overalls, usually of white duck or denim, with a detachable nail pouch at the waist. These were specially made overalls with straps and pockets to hold working paraphernalia. One such overall of the 1920s had 13 special pockets—four nail pockets, two front pockets, three pencil pockets, two hip pockets, one watch pocket, a rule pocket, a hammer loop, try square loops, and a screwdriver loop. The carpenter of that period wore a durable work shirt as well.

Times have changed. Today the average carpenter wears ordinary work clothes, usually tough cotton jeans that can withstand many washings. Her or his tools are generally inserted in loops located either in the nail pouch or in a heavy leather belt worn around the waist.

For protection from job hazards, the carpenter wears safety shoes or sturdy high-top work shoes. (On many construction jobs, safety shoes are required.) He or she also wears a hard hat and, when handling certain power tools, will use a set of safety goggles or a visor to protect the eyes.

If it's the first day on a particular construction job, the carpenter usually brings tools along—clean, sharp, and orderly—in a toolbox. A carpenter takes great pride in her or his tools, protecting them from rust with frequent oilings, and checking the handles and making sure they are securely fixed to their metal shafts. A mental inventory of the toolbox's contents is taken at the end of the day to make sure that all the tools are there.

Many carpenters develop a special fondness for certain basic tools and can tell you when and how they were acquired. They will speak with pride of their tools' quality and usefulness. Recognizing this trait, building contractors encourage carpenters, millwrights, and other construction workers to use their own tools. However, the contractor is still expected to supply the necessary power tools. All journeymen carpenters are skilled in the use of saber saws, radial saws, and other small power devices.

Most major contractors are also expected to provide facilities for locking up tools at the job site overnight. This way the carpenter simply goes directly to the toolshed when the workday begins. Vandalism is sometimes a problem in remote, poorly protected job sites, however, and the carpenter with expensive tools usually takes special precautions. The contractor, nevertheless, is expected to provide a toolshed; most carry insurance to cover losses of tools and equipment.

In some residential construction and highway or bridge construction, the workers often have to take their tools home each night and return with them each morning. The trunks of cars or the backs of pickup trucks become their portable tool supply.

On the job, carpenters work steadily to keep pace with their fellow workers. Blue-collar construction workers have coffee breaks like white-collar office workers. The work breaks occur depending on the availability of building supplies, whether concrete is pouring or not, and other factors. Consequently, many carpenters bring their own thermos bottles of coffee and take breaks when they can.

They usually bring lunch from home, too, unless there is a lunch stand, counter, or "wagon" nearby. Hard work brings a healthy appetite, and the carpenter eats heartily.

Many years ago, steam whistles started and stopped work on major construction projects. Custom and city-noise ordinances have eliminated most of the whistles, and the workers simply knock off for lunch and sit around on stacks of lumber or toolboxes.

WHO IS BOSS ON THE JOB?

An important part of an apprentice carpenter's learning process is her or his on-the-job training. An apprentice is assigned to work under an experienced journeyman carpenter, so that he or she will pick up skills by watching and emulating. This journeyman is the apprentice's immediate boss.

The journeyman carpenter's immediate supervisor is the foreman—another experienced journeyman who directs the work crew of carpenters and indicates what is to be accomplished each day. Over the foreman is the superintendent, who supervises the work of all crafts and is answerable to the contractor.

Teamwork counts in building construction, where the job must be done on schedule. The carpenter works with engineers, architects, and subcontractors, as the job requires.

Many members of the craft work in shops and mills where the workday is fixed (except for occasional overtime). Unless there are big orders to be completed on short notice, the cabinetmaker or millwright in such employment works a regular thirty-five- or forty-hour week. In building construction, however, the carpenter can often expect to work hard for short periods when contractors are struggling to meet deadlines. Since contractors may have to pay penalties when they do not complete projects on time, they may sometimes require carpenters to work overtime.

DAYS WITHOUT WORK

Since some carpentry work is seasonal and building supplies do not always arrive on schedule, there are days when there is no work.

When carpenters, cabinetmakers, or millwrights are laid off or have finished work on a particular job, they may check in with their local union, if they are union members, to let the union business agent know they are available for other work. They then go on a waiting list, if there is one, or they can visit the union hall—usually early on a Monday morning—to pick up new jobs.

Contractors learn to ask for specific journeymen with whom they have worked before. A good carpenter can nearly always find work.

If the carpenter is not a union member, he or she may scan the classified ads, call fellow construction workers for leads, or visit construction sites. The nonunion carpenter finds most of her or his work in residential construction, in maintenance work, or in small commercial construction, where union representation is weak.

Some carpenters change employers each time they finish a construction job. Others alternate between working for a contractor and working as contractors themselves on small jobs. It has been estimated that one out of three carpenters is self-employed at some time during her or his career.

SPECIALTY WORKDAYS

We have described the working conditions of the construction carpenter. Similar conditions exist for skilled workers under the broader definition of carpenter—pile drivers, dockworkers, shipyard carpenters, and so on.

There are situations, of course, where part of the workday involves the difficulties of getting to the job site—which might be by boat, by tramway to a mountaintop, or even by plane or helicopter to some remote spot.

Under any conditions, the carpenters, cabinetmakers, pile drivers, millwrights, and other allied workers perform gratifying, creative, and lasting work. For most of them, no two days are exactly alike. They can point with pride, years later, to a building, bridge, or highway they once helped to build.

There is a growing awareness among the general population of the important role played by carpenters and other building tradespeople in our society. When the beautiful East Building of the National Gallery of Art in the nation's capital was opened to the public in June 1978, one of the VIP openings that preceded the event was a special reception for the workers who had built the gallery. It was out of respect and admiration for their skill and devotion that the noted architect I. M. Pei and the gallery's former director, J. Carter Brown, felt it appropriate to pay homage to the men and women of the building trades.

CHAPTER 3

THE CARPENTER IN THE 21ST CENTURY

Some of the spectacular things that are happening in the world of science and technology will undoubtedly change the work, and the lifestyle, of tomorrow's carpenter. Scientists are striving to improve life on earth through better shelters, climate controls (solar heat and thermal exchanges, for example), new ways of distributing food and clothing, and through newly developed communications systems.

They are plumbing the ocean depths for new ways to harvest the undersea world and for better methods of installing new structures under the waves.

They are sending forth manned and unmanned spacecraft on missions of exploration that may eventually lead to space stations linking this planet with outposts elsewhere in the solar system.

It is not far-fetched to imagine that many young people entering carpentry today will someday be in the vanguard of such fantastic developments.

NEW TECHNIQUES AND TOOLS

There are already clues to tomorrow's work style. The laser beam, that intense ray that seems to come right out of science fiction, is already being used to a limited extent in surveying job sites. With micrometer accuracy, a laser beam helps a millwright set an atomic reactor precisely. It also helps carpenters and pile drivers align pilings for docks during the long winter nights in Alaska.

New adhesives are taking the place of tacks and nails in many applications. Based on formulas developed for the space program, many of these adhesives work in all kinds of temperatures, above water, under water, and under pressure.

Basic tools, too, are being modified and improved. When astronauts needed special hand tools for their routine chores in space capsules (where they worked in tight spaces and in weightless conditions), science developed special tools that may now have applications on earth.

New building materials also are coming to the fore each succeeding decade, as chemists explore new possibilities of the raw materials. We have new laminations, new foam substances, new superhardeners, and so on. As each new product comes into the construction market, the carpenter must learn to work with it. We have new types of insulation, new floor coverings, and new ways of impregnating wood. Carpenters will undoubtedly always work with wood, as science learns to better conserve and harvest this basic resource, but they will work with scores of new materials as well.

HOUSING AND CITY PLANNING

As the United States changed from a predominantly rural society to a highly concentrated urban society in the twentieth century, carpenters found themselves working in planned communities, satellite cities, and residential cul-de-sacs.

As building codes, government financing, and city planners moved more and more into construction work, carpenters found themselves dealing less and less with custom construction and more and more with mass housing and major commercial construction. Experts in the industry expect these trends to continue.

As sources of energy became scarce in the twentieth century, Americans began to change their thinking about mass transportation. We can expect to have much emphasis placed on mass transit in tomorrow's cities, and carpenters will be building subways, subway stations, perhaps even monorails as well as other systems for the mass movement of people.

TO THE OCEAN'S DEPTHS

Some carpenters and millwrights are employed on the offshore drilling platforms along our coasts. Occasionally, pile drivers have donned undersea gear for their work in some phase of dock construction.

As scientists talk of year-round communities under the sea for the dredging of minerals and the developing and harvesting of fish, carpenters may be working in underwater airlocks.

Researchers have already proven that it is feasible to live for periods of several weeks in underwater homes on the continental shelf.

MORE GIANT STEPS IN SPACE?

Although the costs seem almost insurmountable today, there may be a time when human civilization will extend its realm to the moon and beyond—with solar stations, mining facilities, and research stations on the earth's only natural satellite. In such cases, tomorrow's carpenters may wear spacesuits as they go about their work.

CHAPTER 4

IS CARPENTRY FOR YOU?

Carpenters, to be successful, must be able to work with their hands as well as their heads. They are creative persons who like to use specifications, drawings, and tools to create something new and useful.

Carpenters find plenty of action and variety in their work. They take pride in their skills and in doing their jobs well.

PROFILE OF A CARPENTER

The late novelist Edna Ferber had warm words for the carpenter in her book, *A Kind of Magic.*

> There is a rare characteristic inherent in men whose guild or craft is that of carpenter. I have occasionally known and remonstrated with surly, unreliable and careless workmen of just about all other crafts and trades. I never have known a genuine carpenter who was not prideful in his work; gentle, forthright and humane in his nature. Carpenters are, mysteriously, likely to be men of intelligence and integrity; they are at once visionary and realistic. Perhaps the working with wood has something to do with all this. Sawing, cutting, hammering, nailing, the scent of clean wood is always in his

> nostrils. Perhaps still lurking in the wood is something of the quiet fragrant forest whence it came. It just could be that the still-living tonic of the long-felled trees clears the workman's brain and steadies his nerves and makes his hand sure and deft. Carpenters talk little above the tap of the hammer, the buzz of the saw, but, when they do speak, they are likely to be unloquacious and dryly humorous. All this fancied explanation could be false—and probably is. Doubtless the fundamental explanation for the characteristics of the genuine carpenter is that he is descended from the carpenter who possessed all these qualities—the carpenter craftsman, Jesus Christ.

You don't need exceptional physical strength to be a carpenter, but you must be healthy enough to lift many types of building materials, agile enough to climb ladders and maintain a good balance on scaffolds, and tough enough to work under occasional adverse weather conditions. You should also have a high tolerance for noise; on a construction site, a carpenter hears the pounding of hammers and the buzz of power tools almost constantly.

CARPENTRY TRAINING AND EDUCATION

Although a high school diploma is not absolutely essential, it is desirable and is still required for some apprenticeship training programs. Experienced apprenticeship instructors and vocational teachers are finding, however, that aptitude, manual skills, and a knowledge of basic mathematics are all that are needed to launch a young person into a carpentry training program. In many areas, a high school diploma is not as important as a natural ability to work with tools and to understand and apply the rules of arithmetic.

However, in some areas where carpentry training is offered, the applicant for training must be a high school graduate or possess an education equivalency certificate. Transcripts of school records may be requested. Check school officials for the requirements in your area.

Students entering the job market right out of high school without some plan for vocational or specialized training sometimes find the employment situation discouraging. Many of these graduates have serious skill deficiencies in three basic areas: communications, mathematical skills, and problem solving. It was estimated that more than half of the seventeen-year-olds in high schools can't solve a math problem involving several steps before reaching a solution. With math and problem solving of major importance in carpentry, it is vital that a person pursuing this vocation give special attention to learning basic math while in school.

The young person with a serious interest in carpentry must keep her or his sights on long-range goals and not be tempted to quit training for quick money at some other job that can be more easily learned.

THE FUTURE BELONGS TO MEN
AND WOMEN OF SKILL

A philosopher once said, "The man who has a trade has an estate." He was not speaking of real estate, but rather underscoring the fact that people who have specialized knowledge, skills, and experience have more than money. They have a guarantee of future income. Their vocation becomes an estate.

The minimum age for admission to a carpentry apprenticeship training program is seventeen. There is no upper age limit, so people can apply in their twenties, thirties, and so on.

Once you become a journeyman—a full-fledged carpenter—you may work as a journeyman all your life and be assured of a vocation that is always in demand. There is no official retirement age. The age of retirement depends upon the individual, the employer, and the individual's ability to do the work well.

The journeyman carpenter also may elect to move to other jobs such as estimator, inspector, foreman, or superintendent—or even to the ownership of a contracting business of her or his own.

Several years ago, for the first time, the number of white-collar workers in this country surpassed the number of blue-collar workers. Automation and increased technology have reduced the number of unskilled workers needed in many plants and industries. The most experienced and skilled industrial workers are kept on until last, but even they sometimes are laid off, as the machines perform more complex tasks.

The blue-collar carpenters and their fellow construction workers, however, will continue to be needed because of their special skills. Society will always need its builders.

Along with this continued need for skilled craftspeople has come a rise in the social status of the carpenter. In studies made by a group of sociologists over a forty-year period, carpenters rose from sixteenth place to eleventh place in preferred occupations.

WHAT TO EXPECT IN FINANCIAL RETURNS

One big advantage in learning to be a carpenter is that you draw pay from the first day you begin training as an apprentice. Once

· you are accepted in an apprenticeship or pre-apprenticeship training program, you are both a student and an employed worker.

In most areas, the apprentice's starting wage is approximately 40 percent of the journeyman wage scale, and the wage is increased periodically, usually every six months, until the apprentice is earning 90 percent in her or his fourth and final year of apprenticeship training.

To find out what the pay is in your particular area, you need to know the current wage scale of journeymen carpenters, at what percentage of the scale apprentices are started and advanced, and how many months are required for each period of advancement. The local carpenters' union office can give you this information.

In the mid-1990s, according to the U.S. Bureau of Labor Statistics, the median weekly salary, not self-employed, union and nonunion, was about $476. Weekly earnings for the top 10 percent of all carpenters was more than $900. The lowest 10 percent earned less than $300. Earnings may be reduced on occasion because carpenters lose time in bad weather and periods of recession when jobs are less available. By the year 2000, the median weekly salary is expected to rise to more than $600.

Fringe benefits paid by an employer (hospitalization, retirement, and so on) sometimes add to the take-home pay.

The average number of hours people work per week in the various specialty trades of carpentry varies somewhat, according to the Bureau of Labor Statistics. Carpenters, overall, put in 39.1 hours per week; residential carpenters, 37 hours; floorcoverers, 35 hours; and highway and street carpenters, 45 hours. (Under most union contracts, carpenters receive overtime pay for all work over either 35 hours or 40 hours, depending upon what has been negotiated.)

In addition, the carpenter receives overtime premium pay for all work outside of normal working hours and premium pay if he or she does hazardous work. In some instances, particularly when they work under a contract or for an employer year-round, carpenters also receive health and welfare benefits, pension benefits, and paid holidays. Under some union contracts, carpenters can acquire credits toward vacation pay from contractor associations. Maintenance carpenters employed on a year-round basis can expect vacations and holidays with pay.

Much is said in the press about the high wages paid to union construction tradespeople. It is true that construction workers, including carpenters, get relatively good hourly wage rates under union-negotiated contracts, and they are, over the long haul, achieving gains in fringe benefits. What so much of the public fails to realize, however, is that, under present circumstances, the average construction worker does not work every possible workday of every year. In other words, her or his annual income is not what it would be if steady work were available year-round.

This is because seasonality is a problem in the construction industry. Projects are sometimes shut down because of bad weather or a short supply of materials, because funds have not been appropriated for a project, or for other reasons. The months from April to November are the busiest for outside carpenters.

Union construction workers could achieve annual incomes of $50,000 and more if problems of seasonality could be overcome and carpenters were able to work year-round. As it is, some achieve only $10,000 in bad economic years and in periods of unusually bad weather.

Carpenters expect some loss in pay while changing from one building project to another or during layoffs because of seasonality. However, steady work is usually guaranteed for the most competent workers because they are so valued by their employers.

Recently, technological changes in the industry have boosted its ability to provide continuous employment. Thanks to this aspect, many firms are now able to carry on assembly and fabrication of components in their shops during temporary declines at the job site.

WHAT AUTHORITIES SAY

"We need to double and even triple our number of apprentices," a former general president of the United Brotherhood of Carpenters and Joiners of America told a gathering of union and management training leaders. He called upon employers and contractors to employ more apprentices, estimating that if each employer added just one apprentice to the payroll, the number on the job would nearly triple.

The administrator of the U.S. Department of Labor's Bureau of Apprenticeship and Training has stated that present registrations of apprentices in the building trades are not enough: "The years ahead are going to present a great demand."

The chairperson of the Manpower Task Force of the National Association of Home Builders recently told graduating carpenters and apprentices, "You have, by great wisdom or happenstance, chosen a career in the construction industry which offers great promise for you in the future." He cited population figures and federal expenditures to support his optimism.

THE STATUS OF THE CARPENTER

If social status has any bearing on your chosen vocation, the carpenter stands pretty high among those who work with their hands and, as a matter of fact, in the overall job picture.

Back in 1925, a fellow named George S. Counts became concerned about the prestige of the teaching profession. He felt that young people of the Roaring Twenties were disregarding the social status of certain occupations when they chose their life's work, and he decided to make an inquiry into the social status of various occupations. With no network of pollsters to assist him, he nevertheless drew up a list of twenty-five occupations (from army captain to waiter) and asked five groups of high school and college students—368 students in all, plus 82 schoolteachers—to number 1–25 their judgments of the most socially important vocations.

There was a great deal of agreement among the various groups polled on a well-defined prestige order, running from banker to ditch digger. While the farmer and the grocer were higher up the ladder, the carpenter was still number sixteen in the final vote—third only to the machinist and the electrician among blue-collar workers.

Twenty-one years later, just after World War, II, two social researchers, M. E. Deeg and D. G. Paterson, decided to take another poll on the same subject. They mimeographed a survey sheet and distributed it to 191 male and 190 female undergraduates enrolled in introductory psychology courses at the University of Minnesota. Deeg and Paterson's survey showed little change from the Counts poll of twenty-one years before. The carpenter, however, moved up to fifteenth place.

Then, in 1967, three more University of Minnesota researchers decided to make still another twenty-one-year-cycle survey. Hakel, Hollmann, and Dunnette published their findings. This time, the carpenter jumped from fifteenth to eleventh in the ratings.

The results of this survey indicate improved standards of living for those ranked lower on the social scale and more respect for those employed in blue-collar work.

    Recent indications are that many college graduates are turning to carpentry and the building trades—for the dignity of the work and the satisfaction and pay.

CHAPTER 5

PREPARING FOR A CARPENTRY CAREER

If you have ambition and an aptitude for carpentry, a high school education is desirable but not absolutely essential. In nearly all carpentry training programs, however, you must have successfully completed at least two years of high school.

Today, there are so-called pre-apprenticeship programs sponsored by public and private agencies that help a person brush up on language and math basics. Such programs are especially valuable for school dropouts. In recent years, employer organizations and unions have relaxed the educational requirements somewhat, so that more young people, particularly high school dropouts, will have a chance to acquire a vocation.

Nevertheless, a high school diploma would, of course, be an asset in achieving advancement in the industry, and high school mathematics is essential. Mechanical drawing and shop courses also offer long-range advantages.

In any case, it will be difficult to obtain sufficient training and experience outside an apprenticeship training program. These programs are usually cosponsored by labor and management groups under joint apprenticeship training committees.

The National Joint Carpentry Apprenticeship and Training Committee, a labor and management group that works with the U.S. Department of Labor, prepares and approves apprenticeship standards for carpenters and all the other various specialties included in the carpentry trade. The purpose of these standards is "the establishment and maintenance of high standards of the trade and the development of skill and knowledge of the apprentice." They are also designed "to assure the continuance of the development techniques, standards of practice, and workmanship, to give vitality to them, to promote uniformity of practice..." These standards are considered as basic requirements for journeymanship, regardless of local conditions.

The educational requirements under each of these standards read as follows: "Applicants for apprenticeship shall satisfy the local joint committee that they have sufficient education to take the related instruction..." That is all. So a high school diploma is not required, but certainly it would be an excellent way of satisfying a local labor-management training committee.

HIGH SCHOOL PREPARATION

The traditional courses that prepare a young person for a career in carpentry are:

Mathematics. A good comprehension of basic mathematics is essential. A knowledge of how to reduce fractions to their lowest terms and how to multiply and divide numbers with decimal points is required for most apprenticeship qualifying tests in this vocation. You may be able to forget some of the so-called "new" and theoretical math, but you must be prepared to figure the amount of building materials needed for a construction job. You must learn something of simple geometry, so that you can determine the pitch of rafters, for example, or work with data obtained by a transit survey.

Mechanical Drawing and Industrial Arts. Many high schools are making changes in their vocational training curricula, placing less emphasis on what might be considered do-it-yourself projects, such as the creating of broom holders and bookshelves, and more emphasis on an overall understanding of the construction industry. Mechanical drawing and drafting are becoming part of this overall training course.

A carpenter is expected to be able to read blueprints. He or she gets such training during the apprenticeship, but the better prepared a young person is to start carpentry apprenticeship training, the more time he or she will have to absorb the more difficult elements of carpentry.

Generally speaking, high school industrial arts courses will help young people discover whether or not they want to be carpenters by exposing them to some of the basics of working with tools. However, this exposure cannot be considered training in the craft itself.

Other High School Courses. Although no high school courses except mathematics, mechanical drawing, and industrial arts are directly related to carpentry, it is important to realize that employers and labor-management training groups look favorably upon the young person whose overall high school record reflects a variety of interests and talents.

TRADE SCHOOLS

There are a good many vocational training schools spread all across the country that offer courses in carpentry. There are also correspondence courses in the trade. And many mail-order publishers offer sets of books that contain the basic instruction for carpentry.

Some of these courses and books can be used to supplement instruction in preparing for the carpentry trade, but you must remember that there is no substitute for experience—using tools of the trade—in learning a skilled craft.

The best training in carpentry, therefore, comes in working beside and under skilled journeymen and supervisors on the job, which is what an apprenticeship training program offers.

While it is possible to go to a trade school that teaches carpentry and get a certificate that makes you eligible for some jobs in the field, such jobs are limited. When skilled carpenters are needed, most major contractors hire graduates of apprenticeship training programs.

Some private career schools or trade schools take pride in the fact that they graduate students in less than two years. Accredited schools of the National Association of Trade and Technical Schools have courses that last 102 weeks. Union-oriented schools, however, contend that the higher-paid union apprentice is better served with the four-year program.

PRE-APPRENTICESHIP

During the 1970s, in order to offer a helping hand to those young people who could not otherwise bridge the gap between limited education and craft jobs such as carpentry, the federal government launched the first of its manpower training programs. Under the current program, funds are made available to sponsoring organizations to operate pre-apprenticeship training programs.

Under these programs, young people with insufficient education in reading and arithmetic are enrolled in classroom courses in more than a dozen training centers and are paid small amounts while they study. The goal is that when they finish pre-apprenticeship training they will be sufficiently prepared to begin apprenticeship training.

The pre-apprenticeship programs to date have experienced many dropouts. Young people who are not otherwise prepared for apprenticeship, but who stick to their studies while classmates drop by the way, will undoubtedly find opportunities in apprenticeship training waiting for them later on.

Pre-apprentices are paid while they are undergoing training. Sometimes it is the minimum wage, while in some areas it is a percentage of journeyman's pay, slightly above the minimum wage. Under some pre-apprenticeship programs, enrollees undergo a test period or probationary period of two weeks to determine how sincere they are in wanting to get into apprenticeship.

In a few instances pre-apprentices are paid only a flat salary, and in some cases they are provided health and welfare benefits under a union contract just like their journeyman teachers.

WORK AS A CARPENTER'S HELPER

The ratio of apprentices to journeyman carpenters is controlled in some areas by a joint commission of representatives of the local unions and state apprenticeship board, as well as by labor-management agreements. A ratio of one to three is common in some areas and one to five in others. According to the *National Standards Manual,* these ratios should be determined by the localized needs.

In some areas there is strong competition for the available apprenticeships. The young person who wants to enter carpentry apprenticeship should find out whether or not there is a waiting list and, if so, how long it is.

Sometimes a young person who aspires to be a carpenter can take a nonunion job as a carpenter's helper—which is classified as unskilled labor—until an opportunity to enter apprenticeship opens up. However, the union does not recognize the job classification "carpenter's helper," and such work does not replace formal apprenticeship training.

WHY APPRENTICESHIP?

Apprenticeship training is like playing on the scrub team before you're ready for the varsity, like pitching in the bush leagues before you make the majors, like serving an internship before you become a doctor. You would not want your home or your school built by amateurs. You want experts who know how much stress a ceiling beam will take; or who can adequately weatherproof a structure against winter winds and summer rains.

Apprenticeship training as a means of passing on craft skills goes back centuries to early recorded history. It is still practiced to some extent in many trades; for example, in the "needle trades" of the garment industry. Although it is not formalized as it is in the crafts, it also exists for copilots training to be senior pilots of airlines, among instructors hoping to become professors, and among countless other professional groups. It has, through centuries of experience, proven the surest way to prepare a young person for the building and construction trades.

CHAPTER 6

CHOOSING A SPECIALTY

The most familiar work classifications in the carpentry craft are carpenter, cabinetmaker or mill man, and millwright. There are others, including resilient floor layers, interior systems installers, lathers, bridge and dock carpenters, pile drivers, wood turners, and boatbuilders.

Under the jurisdiction of the United Brotherhood of Carpenters and Joiners of America there are, in fact, more than a hundred job classifications. Some are industrial jobs, some are considered unskilled, and some are semiskilled. There are, for example, thousands of lumber and sawmill workers who are members of the Carpenters' Union, and many of their jobs require little or no advance preparation before going to work as full-fledged employees.

We are concerned here only with those jobs that require apprenticeship training, to either a full or limited extent, and that offer good pay scales as journeymen. Let us examine them.

THE GENERAL CARPENTER

The largest number of carpenters are in construction work (as compared to maintenance, remodeling, and so on). These are the "do-all" craftspeople who are skilled in "rough" work, as in concrete-form building and in "finish" work, as in installing cabinets and hanging doors.

As circumstances and ambition permit, carpenters can devote their careers to a specialty or to general work. It depends upon their personal preferences and abilities whether they work at rough framing or forming, decking or roofing, precision layout with blueprints and instruments, or finishing such as installing partitions, wallboard, stairways, windows, and doors. There are also many types of construction to choose from—office buildings, factories, warehouses, theaters, shopping centers, and others.

The largest number of construction carpenters—an estimated 60 percent—go into housing construction. As more and more people move to urban centers, the nation has an increasing demand for adequate housing. The beginning carpenter should be warned, however, that there is a tendency in this critical area for contractors to hire many so-called "scab" or "jackleg" carpenters for the semiskilled "rough" work. Home construction sites are so varied in size and geographic distribution that they often present problems for union organizers seeking to enlist members. In areas where union membership is not strong, wages tend to be lower than in well-organized areas.

Generally, construction carpenters share hard but satisfying work. It is physical work, often out-of-doors. For those persons who like to travel, carpentry skills offer an opportunity to go to the many different areas of the nation and world where such skills are needed. The carpenters, in such cases, obtain "clearance" from their local union into the local union in the area to which they move.

Although the age of wooden ships is past, general carpenters are employed in today's shipyards—building ways, making repairs, doing trim work, and performing many other tasks. They are also employed in highway construction and bridge building.

Many carpenters find work in remodeling and maintenance. Most large industrial plants have either full-time construction craftspeople to perform repair and maintenance tasks or contractual arrangements with outside firms to perform such work.

However, residential and commercial construction are still the major activity of the general carpenter. And now that we've covered some of the many options available to a general carpenter, let's examine the jobs of some of the various specialists.

THE CABINETMAKER

Mill-cabinet work is a highly skilled occupation calling for patience and precision. Once a craft of small shops and independent tradespeople, it is also, today, an assemblage of craftspeople employed in outside work crews, mills, and factories.

In these factories, modern tools and jigs and assembly-line methods allow continuous production of high-quality residential, office, and commercial fixtures.

A career in cabinetry requires patience and exacting skill. It requires much indoor work and offers a variety of specializations. Because the work is indoors, it offers a greater opportunity for steady work than do many general carpentry tasks.

Today, skilled cabinetmakers and millworkers are employed in prefabricating cabinet units and fixtures in plants that are often far away from the site of the cabinets' or fixtures' final installation.

THE MILLWRIGHT

Another craftsperson of precision is the millwright, who is concerned with the precision-fitting of machinery to specifications of thousandths of an inch. It is the millwright who installs and aligns heavy industrial machines so that they operate efficiently. He or she uses micrometers (a precision measuring device) and electronic sensors to install machinery and to connect power-unit shafts to operating equipment.

The millwright installs conveyor systems, escalators, electric generators, and even the big cyclotrons of the atomic age. A nuclear power plant is huge, but millwrights align its working units to specifications similar to those in fine watchmaking.

Though millwrights constitute only a small part of the membership of the United Brotherhood of Carpenters and Joiners of America, the union covering their jurisdiction, they are an elite and skilled group of workers.

Apprentice millwrights spend 144 hours in classes per year, studying the use, maintenance, and calibration of delicate instruments. Their on-the-job training exposes them to the installation of all types of light and heavy metal equipment and machinery. Although much of their work is done indoors, millwrights often work outdoors to install conveyors and power plant equipment.

THE RESILIENT FLOOR LAYER

The installation of fine carpeting, composition materials, and polymer or plastic materials is the work of the resilient floor layer. There is apprenticeship training in this particular skilled trade in a growing number of cities.

In Chicago, for example, apprentices in the resilient floor program spend forty-five days in classroom study of the properties and characteristics of each of the many types of flooring materials.

These apprentices learn to scribe, cut, fit, lay out, and seam tile and sheet stock in a variety of patterns under many different conditions. They learn the skill of binding, cutting, sewing, taping, cementing, and laying carpet as well as how to read blueprints and draw plans. Resilient floor layers' apprentices also learn how to estimate the yardage required for a flooring job. Almost all of their work is indoors, with perhaps the exception of the installation of so-called indoor-outdoor carpets, which may require outdoor work on commercial, institutional, or residential properties.

THE PILE DRIVER

The person who operates the big puffing and pounding machine in the foundation work for a new high-rise building is the pile driver. Pile drivers sometimes work almost entirely alone, once the piles (long shafts made of wood, steel, or concrete used to support great weights) are placed in position for driving into the ground.

The work is outdoors, and it requires steady concentration when the pile driving is underway.

Opportunity for work in this specialty is somewhat limited because only a small number of pile drivers can be employed at one time at a job site.

The pile driver must work closely with surveyors and engineers, driving their piles to particular elevations. At times, rock formations and substrata complications test the knowledge and skill of the pile driver. Pile drivers must learn by experience and training the stress and tolerance of the materials with which they work.

THE SHIPWRIGHT

According to the dictionary, a shipwright is "one whose work is the construction and repair of ships," but that is putting a big story in a small nutshell.

Years ago, when all ships were built of wood and were much smaller than today's vessels, the story was simpler than it is today, though the principles and many of the skills remain the same.

Now, shipwrights share their work with metalworkers, but they have retained their responsibility for "shaping the ship," and they still use many of the traditional craft skills.

Shipwrights follow blueprints and ships' plans and sight, plot, and mark reference points and lines on docks and ways (the inclined structures upon which ships are built or launched) to maintain proper alignment of vessels during construction or repair. For this, they use transits, plumb bobs, tapes, and levels. They build keels and bilge blocks, cradles, and shoring for supporting ships in dry dock or on ways.

Shipwrights also position and secure blocking and other structures on dock platforms, according to ship's blueprints, and align a vessel over blocks.

They establish reference points and lines on a ship's hull for locating machinery and other equipment in accordance with a ship's alignment and shape.

If it is required, shipwrights shape, finish, and install wooden spars, masts, cargo booms, and boat booms. They may also fabricate and install furring pieces, aprons, uprights, and other wood framing in a ship, and trim wooden frames and other timbers. They spike or bolt metal fittings, plates, and bulkheads to the wooden parts of a ship and are responsible for building the staging and scaffolding needed for work on ships.

In most shipyards, shipwrights have a four-year apprenticeship. Their training includes all the areas covered by carpentry apprentices, but they must also learn to work with curved and shaped surfaces instead of with the usual straight and square shapes.

Work in a shipyard appeals to a certain type of carpenter. Those who would be happy doing nothing but shop work would probably not find shipbuilding to their liking. Here, workers perform their tasks in the shop and also out on the ways, under ships, and high in the air above the ways.

A shipwright's tools include, besides the modern power tools, the traditional broad axe, adz (a cutting tool used to shape wood), and caulking equipment. Her or his tool kit is a mixture of ancient and modern tools.

OTHER OCCUPATIONS

In addition to those occupations already listed, a carpenter-trainee can become an acoustical tile installer, a carpenter-welder, or a dock worker. Or he or she may become a deep-sea diver, for such individuals are employed in the installation of boat docks and other waterfront facilities and in the erection and operation of offshore oil drilling rigs.

Some persons in the trade even find employment as wood carvers and as wood-inlay specialists. Such occupations, in most cases, are outgrowths of the basic skills acquired in a general apprenticeship training program.

CHAPTER 7

THE ADVANTAGES
AND DISADVANTAGES OF
A CAREER IN CARPENTRY

We have touched upon some of the disadvantages of carpentry—the seasonal layoffs, the occasional work hazards, and, in some instances, the lack of long-range financial security.

We have also indicated that much is being done to overcome these disadvantages. Before another decade is past, it may be that only a small minority of craftspeople will endure some of these disadvantages.

SEASONALITY

In 1968, a Presidential Commission on Seasonality in Construction was established. The panel—which included government, industry, and labor representatives—studied the methods used by other nations, especially Canada, to overcome seasonal work stoppages. They also investigated ways in which materials and supplies could be programmed to arrive at construction sites on time. They were concerned, too, with methods of overcoming traditional policies of construction financing, whereby funds are often made available in the spring or fall, when they might have as easily been made available at another season of the year.

Technological advances of recent years have produced building materials that can be used at higher and lower temperatures, prefabrications that can be made indoors and moved to all-weather erection sites, and such items as space heaters and plastic canopies to protect workers from the elements.

Because of these studies and advances, seasonality should be a less costly problem in the future. Nevertheless, at present the loss of work time due to bad weather remains an important consideration in the building trades, as well as the fact that every construction job ends in two to three years at the maximum. A recent survey of approximately six million construction workers by the U.S. Department of Labor found that only about 43 percent of them worked 50 to 52 weeks out of a year; 30 percent worked 27 to 49 weeks of the year; 18 percent worked from 1 to 26 weeks at full-time; and 9 percent only worked part-time. And seasonality is still a significant problem for workers in the building trades.

ON-THE-JOB HAZARDS

Statistics of the National Safety Council show a slight increase in on-the-job accidents in the building and construction trades in recent years. Part of this rise is due, of course, to increased activity in the construction industry. Hazards certainly do exist, though, and apprentices in the industry are warned to wear safety equipment and to practice safe working habits on the job.

The Construction Safety Act of 1969 and the Federal Occupational Safety and Health Act of 1970 were designed to increase federal safety inspections on major construction projects and to establish safety standards at the state and local levels.

According to the National Safety Council and data supplied by the U.S. Bureau of Labor Statistics, construction workers in 1997 suffered 9.5 nonfatal and/or disabling injuries per 100 construction employees. This is an improvement over 1990 data, which showed 14.1 disabling injuries per 100. The drop is accredited to more emphasis on worker safety under the Federal Occupation and Safety Act. These were injuries "which resulted in lost time, restriction of worker motion, loss of consciousness, or medical treatment beyond first aid." Coal miners, meanwhile, suffered 10.4 injured workers per 100 miners. The highest injury rate was in air transportation, with 14.8 per 100 employees. Contract construction ranked fifth in the order of injury frequency, according to the *Statistical Abstract of the United States,* a report issued annually by the Bureau of the Census.

Fortunately, there are, throughout the United States, laws providing unemployment compensation benefits for persons disabled by work injuries of long duration. Unfortunately, these jobless benefits vary all over the nation—from a high percentage of normal income in Connecticut and Michigan to a figure below the poverty level in Montana and Puerto Rico.

Legislation has been proposed to standardize unemployment compensation throughout the United States, and labor unions and other groups are pushing such legislation.

In any case, a carpenter laid off by work injury, work stoppage, or other cause may apply for either unemployment compensation or disability benefits through state and local employment agencies.

HEALTH AND WELFARE

Today, most carpenters and other workers in the building and construction trades are covered by federal social security. Most full- and part-time workers in the industry are on payrolls that deduct social security.

This is a great improvement over the situation in the late 1930s, soon after the Social Security Act was passed. It took many years of work on the part of the Social Security Administration, labor unions, and other groups to achieve this form of job security for workers in the building and construction trades.

Because of such old-age protection, today's carpenter can look forward to retirement at an earlier age than before. Social security benefits are usually not enough, but they do offer a nest egg which was lacking a few decades ago.

In 1971, to supplement such retirement income, the United Brotherhood of Carpenters and Joiners of America established the Carpenters Labor-Management Pension Fund, which is designed to eventually offer its members continuous pension coverage, no matter where they work. Many local unions and district councils of this organization have negotiated pension programs with local management.

One of the long-sought goals of the construction industry has been portable pension protection. As things once stood, construction workers who were employed by a firm or contractor that covered them with a pension plan could not take this pension protection with them when they moved to another employer. The plan was not "portable." However, under pro-rate agreements that the carpenters' unions are signing with various pension participants, many carpenters are now able to change employers without losing pension protection.

CASUAL WORK OPPORTUNITIES

Carpenters can pick up occasional odd jobs and supplement their incomes. During seasonal layoffs, some carpenters take on remodeling jobs or home repairs. Others turn their skills to advantage by creating lawn furniture, cabinets, and other items.

Craftspeople should remember, however, that there are physical and moral limits to casual work and moonlighting. Too much outside work can, in the long run, shorten a craftsperson's productive life and can deny work opportunities to others.

UNION OR NONUNION

Essentially, a labor union is formed by workers to improve their wages and working conditions and to establish job security. Unions seek to achieve such advantages by negotiating contracts with the members' employers.

The expense of having full-time union representatives, attorneys, and research workers is covered by dues. Union members can judge for themselves what job advantages they get in relation to the amount of dues they pay. Since the union worker puts in fewer hours on the job because of longer vacations and added holidays, the difference is even greater when measured in terms of total compensation-per-hour actually worked.

As we have mentioned previously, there are areas of the construction industry where carpenters are not sufficiently organized to negotiate working arrangements with management. Carpenters working in such areas must judge for themselves the present and long-range advantages of union membership.

CHAPTER 8

HOW TO GET STARTED

An applicant for apprenticeship training must normally be at least seventeen years old.* There is no upper age limit. An applicant must convince the local apprenticeship and training committee that he or she has the ability and aptitude to master the trade and also has enough education to complete satisfactorily the required instruction. The applicant must be physically capable of performing the work of the trade.

A local committee may establish additional qualifications as it deems necessary, but, according to the national standards, "such qualifications must be specific, clearly stated, and directly related to job performance."

The United Brotherhood of Carpenters and Joiners of America and the management groups that work with the union state firmly that selection of apprentices will be on the basis of qualifications alone—without regard to race, creed, color, or national origin.

"All applicants shall be selected on the basis of objective standards and tests provided by the National Joint Carpentry Apprenticeship and Training Committee which permit review after full

---

*Some states will not permit anyone below the age of eighteen to work in construction because of hazardous work laws. In these states, on-the-job training cannot begin until age eighteen.

and fair opportunity for application; and such program shall be operated on a completely nondiscriminatory basis."

MAKING APPLICATIONS

Here's the usual procedure for applying for training. If you live in a large city, you can probably find a carpenters' joint apprenticeship training program. Check your telephone book or call a local carpenters' union and ask where you should apply.

You might also direct inquiries to local contractors or to a field office of the Bureau of Apprenticeship and Training, U.S. Department of Labor. You can refer to Appendix D at the back of the book for a list of these offices. In addition, an office of the state employment service may be a source of information and assistance.

Because of limited facilities and personnel, some apprenticeship training schools cannot accept all applicants as quickly as they would like. Class enrollments are limited. After fourth-year apprentices have completed their work and received their journeyman certificates, each successive class moves up, and there are openings for first-year apprentices.

At least thirty days public notice is given in advance of the earliest date for application for admission to the program. Joint training committees must accept applications over a period of not less than two weeks. All applicants who are placed on a list of qualified eligibles will be retained on the list, subject to selection, for a period of two years.

In some areas, training directors ask applicants to present letters of recommendation from two former employers (if you have two), letters of character reference (usually two), a birth certificate, a training certificate or high school diploma (if you have one), and a military discharge (if applicable).

After your application is checked by officers of the apprenticeship training program, a letter will be sent either to you or to your high school to obtain a transcript of your grades. Upon receiving this request, the high school will mail the transcript directly to the apprenticeship training office.

Aptitude tests are given periodically by many training committees, and you will be notified when you can take a test. The test is designed to show your language and reading ability, your ability with arithmetic used in the trade, and your natural talent for carpentry. Later, you'll be notified by mail whether you passed or failed this test.

An informal interview is arranged by some joint committees to give you full details of the program, inform you of the wages you'll receive during apprenticeship, and offer you other special information. You will be invited to ask any questions you wish during this interview.

If you meet all of the qualifications, you're ready for the first stage of apprenticeship training.

ENTERING THE PROGRAM

A major consideration in getting into a carpentry apprenticeship program is your ability to be placed in on-the-job training. If, by chance, you are able to obtain ahead of time from an employer an *intent to hire,* a statement that will show a local joint committee or training school that a contractor is prepared to hire you as an apprentice, then you have taken a major step toward entering carpentry apprenticeship.

If, however, you go first to the training school or committee, and you pass the preliminary requirements, the school or local union may provide you with a letter of introduction and a list of potential employers. If one of these contractors will agree to hire you, you then return to the union and make appropriate arrangements for work-study.

TERM OF APPRENTICESHIP

The normal term of apprenticeship for the carpentry trade is four calendar years (between 5,200 and 8,000 work hours), consisting of eight six-month periods of reasonably continuous employment, including the probationary period and the required hours of supplemental school instruction. (Note: working a 40-hour week for all 52 weeks of a year would total 2,080 hours of work and training per year. Hence, the 5,200 to 8,000 hour total required. Because of employment uncertainties, training groups are lenient as to total time served.)

The local or areawide Joint Apprenticeship and Training Committee may, through the reevaluation process, accelerate the advancement of an apprentice who shows ability and mastery of the trade to the level for which he or she is qualified. On the other hand, the standard term of apprenticeship may be extended by the local or areawide committee for one year upon satisfactory proof that the apprentice cannot command the minimum scale of wages paid to journeymen.

Apprentice applicants who have had previous creditable training and are experienced in the trade or who have had related instruction may be granted advanced standing on the basis of demonstrated ability and knowledge. If the local committee grants advanced standing, the apprentice shall be paid the rate of the period to which he or she is advanced.

An apprentice agreement is drawn up between you (the trainee) and your trainer or training organization. If you are seventeen years of age, a parent or guardian will be expected to sign your agreement. The document is a protection for you, in that it ensures you of training and preparation for a career as long as you live up to the standards required. It is also a protection for the committee or the employer, because it assures them that you will keep your part of the training bargain.

Apprentices employed under these standards are subject to a tryout or probationary period that should not exceed ninety days of "reasonably continuous employment." This period is designed as a final check on the trainee's fitness for the work.

During any probationary period, annulment of the apprentice agreement may be made by the local joint committee upon written request of any party (including you) for due cause, such as lack of progress or lack of interest.

If, for any reason, you are forced to drop out of an apprentice training program and you reenter it later, you will be given full credit for time served. All claims of previous experience will be evaluated, and you will be paid the wage rate for the training in which you are classified.

ON-THE-JOB TRAINING

When you start in as an apprentice on the job, you will be given a variety of tasks at construction projects. These varied assignments give you the work experience required to cover the wide range of jobs you'll need to know.

Pay for on-the-job work comes from the contractor on the project. Pay scales are based upon the collective bargaining agreement between the union and the area contractors.

Like others in the building trades, carpenters expect loss of work time each time a project is completed, and seasonal dips in work volume. These work fluctuations apply to the apprentice also. However, competent workers are so valued that work is usually available for them.

REQUIRED WORK EXPERIENCE

Carpenter

Following are the approximate hours of work experience you will be expected to put in during your four-year apprenticeship before you become a journeyman carpenter:

Work Processes	Approximate Hours
Layout	325–500
Laying out of batterboards, partitions, doors, windows, and box-out in concrete walls.	
Form building	780–1,200
Building and placing straight concrete forms, irregular concrete forms, concrete forms for stairways, floors, walls, and columns.	
Rough framing	780–1,200
Framing floors, walls, roof, stairs, scaffolding, and so forth on both house and heavy construction. Roof covering.	
Outside finishing	520–800
Applying cornice and wall trim. Setting door and window frames. Applying trimming fixtures.	
Inside finishing	975–1,500
Applying door and window trim, baseboards, and moldings. Fitting and sanding doors and windows. Constructing and setting cases, wardrobes, stair work, and flooring. Applying hardware and fittings	

to exterior and interior of building, doors,
and windows.

Care and use of tools and
woodworking machinery   325–500

Welding.   325–500

Plastics and resilients.   195–300

Acoustics and drywall   650–1,000

A. Ceilings
   Laying out, cutting, assembling, and installing all materials
   and component parts.
   1. Hangers, channels, furring and backing boards.
   2. Bars, main tees, cross tees, splines.
   3. Stiffeners and braces.
   4. Ceiling angles or moldings.
   5. Finish ceiling materials.
   6. Items of local practices.

B. Walls and Partitions
   Laying out, cutting, assembling, erecting and/or applying all
   materials and components parts.
   1. Floor and ceiling runners.
   2. Studs, stiffeners, bracing, fireblocking.
   3. Resilient and furring channels.
   4. Laying out, framing, enclosing, and trimming door frames,
      window frames, vents, light wells, and other openings.
   5. Wall angles and moldings.
   6. Studless and laminated installations.
   7. Thermal and sound insulation.
   8. Installing backing and finish materials.
   9. Fireproofing columns, beams, and chases.
   10. Items of local practices.

Miscellaneous............................	260–400
Scaffolding, walkways, shoring, sheds, safety and protection.	
Asbestos abatement and other hazardous material handling and disposal	65–100
Total	5,200–8000

The apprentice shall also perform such other duties in the shop and on the job as are commonly related to such apprenticeship.

Cabinetmaker

Under present standards, these are the approximate hours of work experience required of a mill-cabinet trainee:

Work Processes	*Approximate Hours*
Sharpening and using hand tools..............	325–500
Working from stock bills and drawings	325–500
Using power equipment, cut-off saws, table saws, jointers, routers, planers, sharpers, and sanders..	975–1,500
Grinding knives and filing saws..............	325–500
Laying, matching, and cutting veneers..........	195–300
Dressing and preparing material for assembly ...	325–500
Gluing stock	130–200
Laying out work for milling and general trimsaw work from stock bills and details	650–1,000

Sanding moldings, gluing flat work and squares, cleaning for finish............................	130–200
Assembling doors, drawers, skeleton frames, fitting and hanging doors and drawers, fitting and applying moldings, matching veneers.......	520–800
Assembling and installing cabinets, built-ins, and paneling.............................	975–1,500
Laying out, machining, and assembling cabinets and built-ins.............................	325–500
Total.............................	5,200–8,000

The apprentice shall also perform such other duties as are commonly related to such apprenticeship.

Millwright

The following schedule is an example of the type of work experience and training considered necessary to develop a skilled and productive worker in the millwright trade. Within the limits of basic trade requirements, the schedule is adaptable to local conditions.

Work Processes	*Approximate Hours*
Using hand, power, bench, and machine tools....	975–1,500
Installing and aligning machines..............	1,300–2,000
Using rigging, welding, and precision equipment..	975–1,500
Using optical instruments and lasers...........	975–1,500

Reading blueprints	455–700
Practicing various types of welding *(arc, MIG, oxy-acetylene, TIG, plastic)*	520–800
Total	5,200–8,000

Wall and Floor Coverer

The floor and wall-covering trade has grown tremendously in recent years, particularly in office-building installations. Apprenticeship standards have been developed for this specialty worker. The following schedule is an example of the type of work experience necessary to develop a skilled and productive worker in the trade.

Work Processes	*Approximate Hours*
Carpeting:	
Handling materials	130–200
Conventional carpet, high density foam-backed, rubberbacked padding, other.	
Surface preparation	162–250
Wood, concrete, walls, other.	
Layout	195–300
Estimating/planning, workroom, job site, patterned, and nonpatterned.	
Seaming	260–400
Preparation/methods, thermoplastic (heat), sewing, wet, other.	

Installing padding 130–200
Stapling, gluing, and taping.

Installing fastening devices 130–200
Tackless strip, tacking strip, other.

Installing carpeting 585–900
Convention (stretching), glue down, and taping.

Finishing................................ 65–100
Metals/vinyls, base, other.

Special installations 130–200
Walls, ceilings, furniture, other.

Installing stairs........................... 195–300
Straight, winders, floating, other.

Safety 130–200
Removal, existing materials, adhesives, power
equipment, and hand tools.

Maintaining tools and equipment............. 65–100

General maintenance and repairing 98–150

Hard Surface:

Handling materials........................ 163–250
Sheet goods, tile, and underlayments.

Surface preparation 325–500
Wood, concrete, walls, drywall, and plaster.

Layout.   325–500
Sheet goods, nonpatterned, pattern matching,
custom insets; tile, square installation, diagonal,
patterns, other.

Fitting material.   650–1,000
Knifing, direct scribing, pattern scribing, other.

Methods of application.   325–500
Adhesives, stapling, taping, nailing, other.

Seaming methods   325–500
Double cutting, underscribing, sealing/welding,
other.

Finishing.   162–250
Cove base, base shoe, metals and vinyls.

Miscellaneous.   325–500
Stairs, treads, risers, stringers and walls.

Safety   162–250
Adhesives—removal, existing materials, asbestos-
backed other; power equipment and hand tools.

Maintaining tools and equipment.   65–100

General maintenance and repairs   98–150

Total   5,200–8,000

WORK EXPERIENCE FOR OTHER SPECIALTIES

Related to the carpentry craft is the skilled work of the men and
women who install ceiling systems and the various modern inte-

rior systems. There is also the work experience needed to become a journeyman pile driver.

Trainees for these specialties are not considered apprentices, are not registered as such, and do not receive certificates of training completion. However, they are required to put in a minimum number of hours of on-the-job training before they are considered competent to ply their special trades. The pile driver must complete between 5,200 and 8,000 hours and the interior systems installer must put in 4,000 hours. They also must receive related classroom instructions to qualify them for all types of work in their particular fields.

Pile Driver

These are the appropriate hours of work experience needed of a pile driver trainee:

Work Processes	Approximate Hours
Tools and materials	130–200
Layout	195–300
Pile driving equipment—hammers, leads and rigs, motors and pumps	325–500
Rigging and signaling	260–400
Driving of piles—wood, concrete, steel, etc	650–1,000
Coffer dams and caissons	195–300
Bridge, dock, and wharf construction	520–800
Heavy timber construction	260–400

Care and maintenance of tools and equipment . . .	130–200
Form building	780–1,200
Rough framing	780–1,200
Welding	325–500
Diving and diver tending	325–500
Miscellaneous—safety, scaffolding, shoring, etc. .	325–500
Total	5,200–8,000

Pile driver trainees get instruction in accident prevention, first aid, safety hazards, and state and federal safety codes. The construction of coffer dams excavations and shoring excavations and the floating of water drivers are explained. In addition, the pile driver must know something about bridge construction, overpasses, underpasses, and dock building.

WORK EXPERIENCE: RELATED TRADE SKILLS

An expanding area of work among today's carpenters is the installation of curtain walls, suspended ceilings, pedestal floors, (floors suspended above a base floor to allow computer cables, etc. underneath), and other innovations of interior designers and architects. In the 1980s some technical schools and apprenticeship training programs sought to establish separate work experience schedules for trainees in this new field. They awarded journeyman certificates to students who completed 4,000 hours of work in this area.

It soon became evident, however, that the basic skills of carpentry are needed by a well-rounded interior systems installer. Because of this, training leaders began integrating interior systems skills into the basic carpentry work experience on an elective basis. They advocate between 780 and 1,200 hours of work experience in this and other specialties for apprentices getting on-the-job training with specialty contractors.

There is a growing number of specialty contractors in the construction industry. To supply skilled workers for such contractors, carpentry instructors have established a more flexible curriculum.

These expanded work schedules, introduced in the 1990s, are similar to the curricula college students use in picking their major subjects of study and their electives. For example, an apprentice working for an interior systems contractor might be required to train in the areas of interior finish, interior systems, lathing, comprehensive skills, and knowledge (such as safety and first aid and the use of the transit, level, and laser and the installation of scaffolding). Such electives might be the trainee's major area of training.

In the interior systems specialty, as in others, the apprentice must remain in his or her specialty area of study until at least 80 percent of the skills and tasks listed by the school in that particular area are accomplished.

The apprentice might elect to complete his or her training in the area of hardwood flooring or exterior finish, because of the need for such skills in shopping malls, casinos, and other commercial structures that call for special interior effects and decor.

The new system of "majors" and "electives" not only provides workers for the new construction technologies, but it produces more employable apprentices and journeymen.

In addition to the interior systems specialty, there are other specialized trade skills that offer career opportunities to carpentry trainees.

There are carpenters who work full-time creating and installing exhibits and displays for trade shows. Every major city and resort area has hotels and exhibition halls where exhibits are installed for convention delegates and trade show visitors. Special skills are needed for assembling and installing the components of an exhibit. Many exhibit components are patented and require detailed instructions for erection. There are pipes and frameworks to be put together and drapes and decorations to be installed. Most require special crates to be built. After a show is over, displays must be dismantled and shipped to new locations.

Among other specialties that carpentry apprentices may pursue at some training schools are cabinet manufacturing and fixture work. These are in addition to the basic training of cabinetmaking.

At the end of this chapter you will find an explanation of the Performance Evaluated Training System, or PETS, which was developed by the United Brotherhood of Carpenters and Joiners of America and incorporated in the National Apprenticeship and Training Standards for carpentry. The PETS program has so-called "skill-blocks" for trainees in the work-experience specialties.

RELATED SCHOOL INSTRUCTION

While the apprentice is undergoing on-the-job training, he or she is also devoting time to classroom study. In some cities, such instruction is highly organized with well-equipped classrooms and highly skilled instructors. The apprentice who is in a training program thus equipped is fortunate and should have no difficulty putting in the required hours of classroom instruction (approximately 144 hours per year for each of the four years of apprenticeship).

In many major cities, including Philadelphia, New York, and Chicago, training leaders work closely with public school officials and are permitted to use public educational facilities for classroom instruction. In Philadelphia, for example, the board of education furnishes instructors as well as classroom space at the Mastbaum Vocational-Technical Annex.

In some isolated areas of the nation, it is impractical to set up related training classes because of the small number of apprentices or lack of classroom facilities. In such cases, the local joint committee and/or similar sponsors may obtain instruction material from the Training Department of the United Brotherhood of Carpenters and Joiners of America that may be used to give supplemental instruction.

Experience has shown that the best school instructors are men and women who have worked at the trade. The United Brotherhood of Carpenters and Joiners of America holds periodic seminars for instructors to brief them on the latest developments in the trade and on proper training methods. Some training programs are operated in conjunction with private or publicly operated trade schools. In such cases, instructors must meet the accepted standards of the trade. In no case can the hours of work and hours of school exceed the maximum number of hours prescribed by state, provincial (in Canada), or federal law for a person of the age of the apprentice.

At the close of each six-month period of study and training the apprentices in some areas must pass an examination in order to advance to the next period. When they pass the last of these examinations, they receive a completion certificate stating that they have successfully completed their training and are qualified to work as carpenters, cabinetmakers, or millwrights, depending upon their particular course of work.

CARPENTRY TRAINING IN CANADA

Training in carpentry and other skilled trades through apprenticeship has much support in the provinces of Canada. Many early immigrants to Canada were from France, Scotland, Germany, Poland, and other European nations where training in the skilled trades is a way of life for young people. Many community colleges of Canada offer vocational training in carpentry. The Maritime Province of Nova Scotia is currently expanding its carpentry training program.

Local unions and councils of the United Brotherhood of Carpenters and Joiners of America offer apprenticeship training under the same basic plan as their counterparts in the United States. For information about their programs, check a local telephone book.

To qualify for labor-management training in Canada, a person needs a tenth-grade education or an equivalency proof. Schools in Ontario and some other provinces offer pre-apprenticeship training, the funds for which are supplied by the provincial government.

There are training school openings for minorities. The school operated by Carpenters Local 27 of Toronto currently trains about 15 percent women and 40 percent overall minorities.

THE PERFORMANCE EVALUATED TRAINING SYSTEM

In the late 1970s the Carpenters' Union developed a new and pioneering method of teaching apprentices, which it calls the Performance Evaluated Training System, or PETS.

PETS basically is a method of teaching certain job processes by means of a step-by-step color-slide presentation. The PETS training method enables apprentices to progress in their education at their own pace. They can study the audiovisual presentation, perform the task described, and, if they and their instructors are not satisfied that they have performed the task well, the apprentices can perform it again and again, accompanied by the slides, until they get it right. PETS training material for millwrights includes audiocassettes with the slides.

Under this system, the instructor becomes a resource person, ready to answer questions and offer advice, but much is left up to the PETS equipment to provide the instruction.

The particular trade—carpentry, millwright, cabinet-making, or floor laying—is divided into various teaching sections. Each of these sections is then further divided into skill blocks. Each block covers the necessary blueprint reading, safety factors, and tool skills necessary for that particular job process.

Advancement under the PETS system is based upon completion of specific numbers of skill blocks. The completion of six blocks entitles an apprentice to an advancement in educational position and usually brings advancement in pay. Early completion of the blocks required in a year does not release the apprentice from the obligation of attending school the required number of hours for that year, but does indicate he or she is ready to move ahead, once the time has elapsed.

CHAPTER 9

WHAT TO EXPECT DURING TRAINING

The applicant who is accepted for apprenticeship is issued a probationary identification card. Upon completion of the probationary period and on being admitted to the union and properly indentured, the apprentice is issued a regular work card. Under national standards, the probationary period is not to exceed ninety days of reasonably continuous employment. In most training programs, the joint committee furnishes apprentices with periodic report cards, which are filled in by the apprentices and forwarded to the secretary of the committee at the end of each period. Unless this report is sent in, no credit for work accomplished will be given. The evaluations usually come at six-month intervals.

The joint labor-management training committee keeps a master record of all apprentice work experience and related instruction. In some cities, the training schools forward testing results and other records directly to the joint committee.

The training committee has certain responsibilities during the apprentice's training period. It must see to it that he or she works with a competent journeyman and that he or she is provided, as much as possible, with continuous employment. If it is impossible for one employer to provide the different types of craft experience necessary to give the apprentice all-round training, or if the employer's business is of such a character as not to permit reasonably continuous employment over the entire period of apprenticeship, the local joint committee may arrange to transfer the apprentice to another employer, who will assume all the terms and conditions of the local standards. No apprentice will be transferred to an employer who has not signed an apprentice agreement.

If either the apprentice or the employer becomes dissatisfied with the other's performance, each party has the right and privilege of appealing to the local joint apprenticeship committee for action or adjustment in an effort to remedy the situation. The decision of the committee is final in all matters not in conflict with approved local agreements and with apprenticeship training standards.

WAGES AND WORKING CONDITIONS

The apprentice is to be paid on a "progressive percentage of the journeyman's wage rate, preferably at six-month intervals, and average not less than approximately 50 percent to 75 percent of the journeyman's rate over the apprenticeship term." These are standards established by the U.S. Department of Labor. During the training period, the apprentice is to expect these wage levels and no more.

The hours of work and the working conditions for an apprentice are the same as those covering journeymen. This applies to overtime work, as well as regular work. However, under recommended standards, no apprentice shall be allowed to work overtime if it interferes with related school instruction.

Apprentices who are absent from work through their own fault are expected to make up such lost time before advancing to the next period of apprenticeship.

The National Apprenticeship and Training Committee urges all local joint apprenticeship and training committees to include in their training standards a provision that states that, in addition to the progressive wage percentage, apprentices are eligible for and shall receive the same fringe benefits provided journeymen under the local labor-management bargaining agreement. It also recommends that wages and benefits be combined when establishing wage determinations for a given area.

ON-THE-JOB SAFETY

Construction sites have experienced a relatively high incidence of accidents. Many men and women from the various trades are working together on these sites, and often their jobs cross paths. There is a daily accumulation of debris, and workers have to watch their step, lest they slip on spilled water, oils, chemicals, and the like.

The necessity of working on temporary platforms and stages, plus individual carelessness, adds to the carpenter's hazards. Often, in major construction, carpenters must work high above the ground, and therefore they must always follow the safety rules of the job.

On most jobs, a hard hat of strong, reinforced plastic and with a sturdy head liner is required, as are hard shoes with built-in reinforcements against weights being dropped on the toes and feet.

Safe work habits are stressed throughout the apprentice training period. Apprentices will learn that horseplay is strictly forbidden in most work situations.

The National Safety Council, the union, and the contractors have safety manuals for training purposes. Some of these are used in classroom instruction. In addition, the alert employer displays posters and warning signs at the job site and enforces established safety regulations.

In 1968, building and construction trade unions played a major role in the enactment of improved federal construction safety laws, which call for the full compliance of the industry with federal and state safety inspections. The apprentice, as well as the journeyman, has a responsibility to call the employer's and fellow worker's attention to hazards on the job.

The National Apprenticeship and Training Standards, as revised in 1990, state that:

> The sponsor shall see to it that each apprentice is instructed in safe and healthful work practices and shall ensure that the apprentice is trained in facilities and other environments that are in compliance with either the occupational and safety and health standards promulgated by the Secretary of Labor under Public Law 91-596, dated December 29, 1970, or state standards that have been found to be at least as effective as the federal standards.

GOVERNED BY NATIONAL STANDARDS

Recognized apprenticeship training programs are governed by standards drawn up by a National Joint Carpentry Apprenticeship and Training Committee, representing the United Brotherhood of Carpenters and Joiners of America, Associated General Contractors of America, and the National Association of Home Builders. The committee works in conjunction with the Bureau of Apprenticeship and Training of the U.S. Department of Labor in preparing the national standards. The up-to-date standards are periodically printed by the United States Government Printing Office in Washington, DC, for distribution to joint apprenticeship and training committees, coordinators, and other leaders of the program.

The tradition of training established and protected by these national standards is the result of many years of work and refinement by people in the field, and represents one of the most respected training programs in a trade discipline in the country today.

CHAPTER 10

SPECIAL AVENUES TO CARPENTRY

In an effort to reduce unemployment among young people, the federal government, in recent years, has appropriated funds through various agencies for job training. During the 1960s, one of the ways it conducted the "war on poverty" was by training young men and women under the Manpower Development and Training Administration (MDTA). Another avenue was the Job Corps, which was established in 1964.

In the mid-1970s, MDTA became, CETA—the Comprehensive Employment and Training Administration. And in 1982 Congress enacted the Job Training Partnership Act (JTPA) to replace, CETA. In the early 1990s, the, JTPA, together with the Job Corps, represented the major federal funding efforts to train young people for jobs.

Finally, in 1998, Congress made more changes in manpower training, enacting the Workforce Investment Act, expanding the Job Corps program, and consolidating the work of related agencies. The Workforce Investment Act replaces the JTPA. It becomes effective in July 2000.

THE JOB CORPS

The Job Corps is a network of training centers all over the United States. It is designed to help the underprivileged and those who have not yet obtained high school diplomas to prepare for careers in many fields such as the automotive trades, cooking, forestry, heavy equipment operations, painting, bricklaying, plastering and cement masonry, clerical skills, carpentry, and many more. Pre-apprenticeship training in carpentry is a big part of the Job Corps' activity at many of its training centers. (For a list of Job Corps Training Centers, write U.S. Dept. of Labor, Washington, DC 20213.)

The Job Corps program helps a young person make up much of what he or she may have missed in high school education. It offers vocational training, and it even offers job placement services for the thousands of young men and women who join the Corps each year.

About 80 percent of the Job Corps enrollees are high school dropouts, and approximately 40 percent come from families on public assistance. Sixty-nine percent are from minorities, and nearly 36 percent are women.

The U.S. Department of Labor reported recently that about 64 percent of Job Corps trainees find jobs after finishing the program, including those who join the armed forces; 17 percent seek further education or training (such as carpentry apprenticeship). Twenty percent are not placed at the completion of Job Corps training.

The Job Corps recruits trainees (which it calls "students") through referrals from various public and private agencies. Joint labor-management apprenticeship committees maintained by unions and contractors refer trainees as do state employment offices. You also may apply directly to the Job Corps, Employment and Training Administration, U.S. Department of Labor, Washington, DC 20213.

Candidates for the Job Corps are screened for aptitude and evaluated at various Job Corps training centers. The evaluation panel usually consists of the center director, the educational director, and the coordinator.

Potential Corps members must have a sincere interest in becoming carpenters, painters, or craftspersons in one of the many skills taught. They must demonstrate an ability to perform simple mechanical operations and meet other general selection criteria.

In 1999, Job Corps members were getting an introduction to carpentry at 58 Job Corps centers—30 Civilian Conservation Centers, 15 Contract Centers, and 13 Forest Service Centers. Funds to operate these centers under the Federal Office of Economic Opportunity come from the Department of Agriculture's Forest Service, the Department of the Interior, and, in eleven cases, the Department of Labor. Instructors and training materials are supplied by the Carpenters' Union and by private industry, with the help of federal funds.

When the Job Corps was launched in the 1960s, some training centers were established in cities, where the trainees were readily available. The Office of Economic Opportunity found, however, that it was best to place Corps members in rural and even wilderness locations, where plenty of space was available, there were few distractions, and projects could be undertaken that would be of value to the public. For example, Corps members build shelters and wayside cabins in the national parks and make repairs to existing facilities in state and federal forest preserves.

Job Corps members come from every part of America. The age of applicants is sixteen through twenty-one. Upon acceptance into the Corps, they undergo fifty-two weeks of instruction. Some of the training is in classrooms and leads to the equivalent of a high school diploma, but equal emphasis is placed on job skills. The job skills training is a combination of craft-related instruction and on-the-job experience. Trainees engage in the construction of real buildings and other structures. They perform all of the work normally done by journeyman carpenters, learning to use a transit and level to lay out buildings, using basic tools for the rough framing, doing interior and exterior finishing and trim. Many of the building projects are for public use on or near the centers. These skills are intended to give the Corps member the aptitudes he or she needs to qualify as a carpenter apprentice (or other skilled labor trainee) at the end of his or her year's training.

All Corps members receive a base pay of $100 a month. Another $100 a month is put aside for Job Corps trainees as a readjustment allowance given to them when they leave the center or complete their training. Meanwhile they are provided with room and board in barracks and mess halls.

Many Corps members are considered "functionally illiterate" when they enter the program. Their reading, writing, and arithmetic skills are poor. The training program is designed to improve these basics as well as their vocational abilities.

The Carpenters' Union—the United Brotherhood of Carpenters and Joiners of America—encourages sincere applicants for apprenticeship training who do not qualify for such training to seriously consider the Job Corps route. If, after counseling with the joint apprenticeship and training committee, the young person agrees, he or she is given a referral card and directed to a local Job Corps screener. If he or she meets the Job Corps criteria for entry, he or she is assigned to a Job Corps Center as near his or her home as possible.

After the young person completes one year's training, he or she may then apply for direct entry into the apprenticeship program.

The Carpenters' Union has been very successful in placing Job Corps graduates into apprenticeship training programs. Since it became involved in the program almost a quarter of a century ago, it has accepted several thousand of these young men and women for apprenticeship training, and they have gone on from there to become full-fledged journeymen carpenters. Others were accepted in millcabinet shops or in modular or prefabrication plants or in others areas of the industry. Some have even become Job Corps instructors.

During one typical twelve-month program, 84 percent of the trainees were placed in jobs as apprentices in the industry, while on their way to becoming full-fledged carpenters.

For a free copy of a brochure describing the Job Corps and how you can join its training program, write: Carpenters Union Job Corps Office, United Brotherhood of Carpenters and Joiners of America, 101 Constitution Avenue NW, Washington, DC 20001.

TRAINING FOR NATIVE AMERICANS

In 1986 the U.S. Secretary of Labor authorized an initial grant of $200,000 to the National Congress of American Indians to help Native Americans, including Native Alaskans and Native Hawaiians, to obtain employment and training. With additional funding, the NCAI established a nationwide telephone hotline for Native Americans that provides information about this program and how grants might be obtained for vocational training.

If you are a Native American and seek more information about this program, contact: National Congress of American Indians, 1301 Connecticut Avenue NW, Suite 200, Washington, DC 20036.

THE VOCATIONAL INDUSTRIAL CLUBS OF AMERICA

What the 4H Clubs and the Future Farmers of America are to young and aspiring farmers, the Vocational Industrial Clubs of America (VICA) are to young people seeking vocational careers—including carpentry.

VICA was founded in 1965 and now has fourteen thousand chapters in public high schools, vocational centers, area vocational schools, and two-year colleges throughout the United States and the territorial associations of Puerto Rico, Guam, and the Virgin Islands. Each career group has its own division within the organization, and each operates at the local, state, and national levels. Students form clubs in their schools within their own occupational area with the help of their instructors. The activity is included as a part of the school curriculum. VICA has fifty-three state associations, including Puerto Rico and the Virgin Islands, with a total membership of more than 244,000 students.

Working with vocational instructors and other school leaders, VICA trains young people in leadership skills and shows them how to apply special craft skills such as carpentry and cabinetmaking toward achieving a livelihood after their school days are over.

This organization holds local, state, and national competitions in carpentry and other crafts and trades, and it holds regular club meetings, publishes a national magazine, and participates in international vocational club programs.

For more information about VICA, write: Vocational Industrial Clubs of America, Incorporated, P.O. Box 3000, Leesburg, VA 22075.

TRAINING IN CANADA

There is a counterpart to VICA in Canada, which has been expanding through the provinces of that nation. It's called Skills Canada, and, since it was launched in 1989, more than one hundred Skills Canada Clubs have been established, with almost two thousand members. Its mission is "to champion and stimulate the development of excellent technological and leadership skills in Canadian youth." Skills Canada is currently spreading to secondary schools in the provinces of British Columbia, Alberta, and Quebec. Designed along the lines of VICA in the United States, Skills Canada has provincial skills competitions for aspiring carpenters, cabinetmakers, and other craft workers. Winners in these competitions have begun to compete in VICA's United States Skill Olympics and in the International Youth Skill Olympics.

For more information about Skills Canada, write to the following offices of the organization:

Skills Canada
   299 Doon Valley Drive
   Kitchener, Ontario

Skills Canada
   1101 Prince of Wales Drive
   Ottawa, Ontario

Skills Canada, BC
   3665 Kingsway
   Vancouver, British Columbia

Skills Canada, PEI
   40 Enman Creek
   Charlottetown, Prince Edward Island

Skills Canada, YUKON
   BSMT 3-5100-5th Avenue
   Whitehorse, Yukon Territory

Note: The United Brotherhood of Carpenters and Joiners of America has local unions throughout the provinces of Canada. Check your local telephone book for their location and telephone numbers.

OTHER AVENUES TO CARPENTRY

The U.S. Department of Veterans Affairs also offers advice and counsel to military veterans' organizations, advising them on how veterans may obtain special vocational training. Veterans are advised to check with the Department of Veterans' Affairs and local veterans' organizations as to the availability of any local programs in carpentry and allied skills.

Army Reserve and the regular military offer a limited amount of training in the skilled trades, such as carpentry. In forty hours of "core training" many army reservists are learning to use electrical and pneumatic tools as well as how to do plumbing and surveying work. They then have an option of taking either forty additional hours of carpentry and blueprint reading or an equal number of hours in electrical wiring and welding.

One way to learn the basics of carpentry is by enrolling in a correspondence course. (Correspondence training must be accompanied by hands-on experience, however.) Such training is offered by the International Correspondence Schools (ICS), one of the largest and most respected correspondence schools in the United States. To learn more about ICS's School of Building Trades, write: International Correspondence Schools, 925 Oak Street, Scranton, PA 18540-9887. (There are fees charged for ICS training.)

Carpentry and cabinetmaking are two skills that are much in demand in the Peace Corps. For those adventurous individuals who would like to become vocational teachers themselves, carpentry becomes an asset for serving the country among the underdeveloped nations of the world. For more information on this agency, contact: Peace Corps, 1990 K Street NW, Washington, DC 20036; 800-424-8580.

CHAPTER 11

PROFESSIONAL ORGANIZATIONS

The only worker organization devoted exclusively to the craft of carpentry is the United Brotherhood of Carpenters and Joiners of America, a trade union founded in 1881. It has headquarters in Washington, DC, on Constitution Avenue just below Capitol Hill.

The United Brotherhood of Carpenters and Joiners of America represents more than three-quarters of a million carpenters, cabinetmakers, millwrights, and other skilled workers in the United States and Canada.

EARLY CRAFT GUILDS

In the year 1333, in London, England, a group of carpenters founded their own labor organization. They called it the Carpenters' Guild of London, and it still exists as one of the oldest social institutions in Great Britain.

The guild required each member to attend mass in mid-winter and to pay dues amounting to one penny per person. The ordinances also provided for attendance at funerals of deceased members and made provision for the guild to pay for the services of poor members. Sick members and those out of work were given assistance.

The Carpenters' Guild of London received a formal charter from the Crown in 1477, and a coat-of-arms was produced. In time, the guilds came to be called companies, and it was as companies that the first carpenters' organizations were formed in America.

It was in historic old Carpenters' Hall in Philadelphia, Pennsylvania, that the First Continental Congress of the American Colonies met in 1774. Carpenters' Hall was built to house the Carpenters' Company of the city, a guildlike group of Philadelphia carpenters whose work ornaments the city. Carpenters in the colonies were master builders. They acted as architects, contractors, and wood craftsmen, advising gentlemen such as Benjamin Franklin and Thomas Jefferson on the practicality of their construction ideas.

Early carpenters' unions scored several "firsts" in the trade union movement of North America. They were the first to establish as a trade principle a "book of prices" for accepting pay for their work "so that a workman should receive the worth of his money." Philadelphia carpenters were also the first to strike for a ten-hour workday. That was in 1791. A century later they led the American labor movement's drive for an eight-hour workday.

The carpenters' unions have come forward in times of war and performed heroic service in the construction of army camps and installations and in providing housing for displaced persons.

The present-day organization of carpenters—the United Brotherhood of Carpenters and Joiners of America—was formed in a small union hall in Chicago, Illinois, on August 12, 1881. This date appears on the official seal of the union today. The union is one of the oldest in the American labor movement.

The first meeting of the union did not get much attention in the newspapers of the day. The *Chicago Tribune* noted that "the Knights of the Bench and Sawbuck" were meeting at 192 Washington Street. Much of their time was spent in developing a constitution.

Originally, there were thirty-six delegates from fourteen local unions in eleven cities, representing 2,042 carpenters. They came from Cleveland, Indianapolis, Kansas City, Philadelphia, Buffalo, Detroit, New York City, Washington, DC, St. Louis, Cincinnati, and Chicago—a good representation of America's growing cities.

In those days a carpenter worked for $2 a day. The average workday was ten hours, and the average workweek was six days.

The young union suffered the tribulations of all labor unions in those days—few members, little funds, and difficulties in organizing. Labor unions had few of the legal protections they enjoy today. Workers could be locked out without cause and were often forced to sign "yellow dog" contracts stating that they would not join a union. Hours were long, and working conditions were often dangerous.

In 1886, when the American Federation of Labor (AFL) was formed, the carpenters were well-represented with a delegation at the founding convention. Two of the top officers of the AFL were carpenters—Peter J. McGuire, first secretary of the Carpenter's Brotherhood and the man generally credited with establishing Labor Day, and Gabriel Edmonston, first president of the Carpenters' Union.

Through the years, the union has grown steadily, until it now has approximately 650,000 members in the United States and Canada. Its headquarters is an imposing five-story structure at the foot of Capitol Hill in Washington, DC, where Brotherhood leaders, researchers, statisticians, attorneys, and educators direct and coordinate the work of a broad organization of almost two thousand local unions that exist throughout the United States and Canada.

The Carpenters' Union is essentially a craft union, as distinguished from an industrial union. This means that the union is made up mainly of members of a particular trade or craft.

Any carpenters, cabinetmakers, or millwrights employed in a large industrial plant are enlisted as members of a craft union.

This craft union is separate from the industrial unions in the plant, which are primarily organized to represent the unskilled workers. In industrial relations jargon, it is said that the carpenters "carve out a craft unit" in the plant. The principal advantage to the skilled workers enlisted as members of a craft unit is that they maintain their wage and benefits level above that of the unskilled worker.

There are instances, however, where the Carpenters' Union has organized a plant on an industrial basis, enlisting every worker eligible for union membership, regardless of her or his skill. This is done primarily to give the advantages of union representation to workers who might otherwise not be covered by a union contract. Union carpenters, for example, have organized entire pleasure-boat factories, prefabrication plants, and so on. They are allowed to do so under jurisdictional arrangements within the AFL-CIO and joint industry boards of labor and management.

Each local union elects local officers, draws up bylaws, and usually elects (funds permitting) one or more business agents. The agents' responsibilities are to deal with management on a day-to-day basis, assign union members to jobs, locate work for them, and operate the union hall.

To be eligible for the benefits of union membership, a member must be in good standing, with dues paid. Dues books or dues cards are carried on the person to indicate membership in good standing.

MANAGEMENT ORGANIZATIONS

The primary management groups in the field are the Associated General Contractors of America (AGC), the National Association of Home Builders, and the Associated Building Contractors, Incorporated, all of which maintain headquarters in the nation's capital. Of the three, the AGC is the largest and strongest.

The AGC, as the only national organization of general contractors embracing all types of construction, has as its primary purposes "to represent and serve as the spokesman for the general contracting industry; to seek to improve construction methods, management and service; to eliminate uneconomical and improper practices; and to build skill, integrity, and responsibility throughout the industry."

As a national organization, with more than a hundred chapters and branches throughout the United States, the, AGC serves both the national and local needs of general contractors.

As its name suggests, the National Association of Home Builders is concerned with residential construction. It has branches and offices throughout the country and is concerned with building codes, the technology of the industry, federal activities in home construction, and so on.

The union and the two management groups described above participate jointly in an international apprenticeship training program. In addition, each independently supports various vocational training activities, including those funded under the Federal Manpower Administration.

The third major organization in the field is the Associated Builders and Contractors (ABC), which has headquarters in Rosslyn, Virginia, and chapters in more than forty states. This management association is made up primarily of "open shop" or what ABC calls "merit shop" contractors and builders, which means that its members are opposed to "closed shop" or "union shop" conditions among their building tradespeople.

There are also in the construction industry contractors and builders who employ both union work crews and nonunion work crews.

ABC supports the Merit Shop Foundation, which is a nonprofit organization that was established in 1971 by a group of ABC builders and contractors "to sponsor research and education to improve the technology and environment of the construction industry."

There are also many specialized management groups in the industry: the National Erectors' Association, the International Association of Wall and Ceiling Contractors, Gypsum Drywall Contractors International, the Crane and Rigging Association, Remodeling Contractors, and others. All are organized as trade associations to improve industry conditions, to deal with government regulations, and to work with employee organizations.

CHAPTER 12

RELATED FIELDS AND
BROADER HORIZONS

Experience in the building and construction industry has shown that the best contractors and supervisors are men and women who have served as journeymen in the industry. Carpenters who have worked at all stages of a construction project—from the foundation work to the finishing touches at completion—are often ideally suited to move into managerial positions. Many go into business for themselves as private contractors.

The young man or woman who wants to go far in the industry may wish to take advantage of postgraduate studies through journeyman training classes or courses in junior or technical colleges.

The following are some of the jobs that may be open to the ambitious journeyman:

The Foreman supervises all journeymen of her or his particular trade on a project. He or she plans work, maintains schedules, and works under the job superintendent.

The Job Superintendent directs all construction functions on small- or medium-size projects or on specific phases of major projects. He or she directs work crews through their foremen.

The General Superintendent carries out directions of the project manager, job superintendents, and subcontractors.

The Project Manager directs all construction functions on large projects, coordinating the work of all units. He or she also establishes schedules, working procedures, and job policies.

The Estimator obtains basic data concerning a proposed construction project, usually from plans and specifications. These data include quantities of materials, the number of hours necessary to perform certain types of work, methods to be used, and equipment required. With the assistance of other members of the contractor's office staff, he or she then computes the cost of construction (which represents the contractor's competitive bid for the job).

The Expeditor maintains construction schedules by reviewing deliveries, scheduling the arrival of materials and workers at job sites, establishing priorities, and obtaining clearances.

The Purchasing Agent determines the most economical source of materials; stores supplies, equipment, and parts; and ensures the lowest price consistent with delivery schedules.

The Office Manager maintains an office to centralize supervisory work on the construction site. He or she keeps records, bills clients, makes up payrolls, and handles mail.

The Engineer takes soil and material samples, tests, plans, surveys, and in other ways researches and offers professional recommendations to the contractor as to the best building procedures. Some journeyman carpenters have gone back to school and prepared themselves for jobs as construction engineers.

The Architect designs the buildings and draws up plans and specifications. Students of architecture in our colleges often spend their summers working construction jobs to become familiar with building materials, and so forth. An apprentice or journeyman carpenter who enjoys design work might consider advanced education in architecture.

OTHER AREAS OF ADVANCEMENT

Most of the jobs just mentioned apply to advancements from general carpentry. Mill-cabinet workers and millwrights can advance to foremen and job superintendents. Cabinetmakers may become shop managers and may even go into business for themselves. Millwrights have also gone into business for themselves, pulling together teams of skilled millwrights to bid on jobs.

WORKING FOR YOURSELF

Americans often dream about "being their own boss" and going into business for themselves. It is possible to achieve this dream through carpentry and the allied trades, but the changeover from wage earner to a self-employed person requires careful financial preparation.

To become a contractor, a journeyman must be prepared to bid competitively with giants in the business and to suffer financial losses due to the seasonal and material-shortage nature of the industry. In many cases, contractors must be bonded against failure to complete the assigned work.

As in all business ventures, good character, self-discipline, experience, and patience are prerequisites to success.

Many contractors got their start by knowing someone in the industry who had faith in their ability and advanced the necessary funds to get them started—or at least co-signed a note with them at a local bank.

Bankers are experienced in dealing with building contractors and can offer sound financial advice to a newcomer in the contracting business.

Small contractors sometimes get started with a single successful bid for a job. They should be prepared to follow up this initial success with bids of a similar size on jobs they are able to complete on time.

Many other journeymen have earned their livelihood through maintenance and repair work in industry and in the home. Such men and women list themselves in the yellow pages of telephone books and in classified advertisements. Their best advertising, however, is usually word-of-mouth reports of jobs well done.

Self-employed carpenters usually acquire their own trucks and maintain complete bins of hand and power tools to prepare themselves for any eventuality.

If you are planning to go into business for yourself, you would do well to study the successes of others, analyze the reasons for their success, and plot your future carefully and with determination. Good luck!

GLOSSARY

Acoustical Material.   Composition board and other materials manufactured in sections and placed upon the ceiling or walls of a structure to absorb sounds or reduce sound reflection and echo.

Acoustics.   Pertaining to sound.

Agreement, Collective.   A contract (agreement and contract are used interchangeably) between a union, acting as bargaining agent, and an employer, covering wages, hours, working conditions, and fringe benefits.

Apprentice.   A learner who is under supervision as to work experience, often with related classroom studies. Completion of the required years of apprenticeship training leads to journeyman status.

Area Differential.   Variation in wage rates between areas or regions of the country for identical work. Also called geographical differential.

Backing Board.   A term used in the installation of acoustical materials. It is applied either to panels or furring strips placed on walls, partitions, and ceilings before acoustical tiles or other facings are applied.

Bar.   In acoustical tile installation, the term is applied to metal bars to which the tiles are affixed.

Blue-Collar Worker.   Production and maintenance workers and construction workers as contrasted to office and professional workers who wear "white collars."

Blueprint.   A reproduction of an architect's or designer's plans by a photographic process in white lines on a bright blue background.

Building System.   Another term for systems construction, whereby materials, labor, prefabricated units, and so forth are scheduled for maximum efficiency in time and costs.

Calibration.   The markings on an instrument in degrees, meters, and so on, that indicate a unit of measurement.

Casual Work.   Work that occurs irregularly, on no fixed schedule.

Channel.   A term used in acoustical tile installation that refers to the angled rods and bars supporting the tiles.

Compensation.   Payment for services and wages.

Component.   A distinct part of a whole, as a transistor is a component of a radio; a stove, a component of a kitchen.

Contract.   A legal agreement between two or more interested parties. This might be between a labor union and the employer, covering wages, hours, working conditions, and fringe benefits. It might also be between a contractor and a builder, covering costs, materials, and construction time.

Contractor.   A person or company who agrees, by contract, to do certain work under specified conditions and prices.

Craft.   An occupation or trade requiring a particular ability or skill.

Craftsperson.   A person who practices a particular trade or skill.

Decking.   Materials used for flooring (usually in an exposed area), as, for example, the roadway of a bridge and the flat-floored roofless area adjoining a house.

Drywall.   Panels of gypsum board, fiber board, plywood, or gypsum plaster erected as manufactured in a "dry operation" as opposed to a "wet wall" or wet plaster construction.

Estimator.   One who calculates the amount of materials needed, the labor necessary, and the general costs of a construction job or installation.

Fabrication. Anything constructed from standardized parts. In construction work, the term is usually applied to components that come to a construction site already prepared for installation.

Finish Work. The fine, sometimes decorative, work involved in the final states of construction, installation, or remodeling, usually of a more highly skilled nature.

Fire Blocking. That type of construction work in which fire hazards are reduced by applying wood blocks between studs to prevent "chimney effect" in the event of fire. The blocks stifle the flow of air and help to smother a fire.

Fixture. Something that is fixed in place; for example, a wall cabinet or a ceiling light.

Foreman. A chief and, usually, a specially trained or more experienced worker, who directs the activity of a work crew.

Form. The framing built of wood, metal, or other material, that serves as a form or mold for poured concrete.

Frame. Something composed of parts fitted together and united. In construction, this usually applies to a wooden frame.

Framing. The process of putting together the skeleton parts of a building. Also, the rough lumber work on a structure, such as flooring, roofing, framework, and partitions.

Free Form. A form that has no fixed specifications; usually a variation from a straight line.

Fringe Benefits. Employment benefits granted by an employer or obtained by labor-management contract that are received over and above the basic wage rate; for example, hospitalization insurance and tool allowance.

Furring. The application of thin wood, brick, or metal to joists, studs, or walls to form a level surface or an air space. To build a separate wall offset from the main wall. Also, the materials used in such work.

Hanger.   A wire or bar used for suspending one object from another, as pipes are hung from a ceiling, or a stirruplike drop support attached to a wall to carry the end of a beam.

Hard Hat.   The safety helmet worn by a worker, which is usually made of hard plastic. The term is also applied to a construction worker.

Inspector.   A person who is employed to examine a project, a work site, or an activity to make sure that standards or policies are being carried out.

Jack Leg.   A slang term for an amateur or unskilled carpenter or other worker.

Joiner.   A wood craftsperson who constructs joints or wood connections. Usually a term applied to the workers in shops who construct doors, windows, and other fitted parts of a structure.

Joint Committee.   In this instance, a training committee made up of labor and management, with public officials who serve as consultants or nonvoting members.

Jointer.   Any of various tools used in making joints; also, a person who unites materials with joints.

Joist.   A horizontal beam used with others as a support for a floor, ceiling, or roof.

Journeyman.   A person who has completed her or his apprenticeship and is entitled to the highest minimum wage rate established for her or his job classification.

Jurisdiction.   The area of work or group of employees for which a union claims the rights to bargain collectively.

Laminated.   Composed of layers of wood, or other building materials bonded or impregnated by resins or other adhesives. Plywood, for example, is created of laminated sheets of wood veneer.

Lath.   Any material that is secured to studs or joists and on which plaster is applied.

Lathe. A machine in which wood or other solid material is rotated about a horizontal axis and shaped by a fixed cutting tool; also, the action of cutting or shaping with a lathe.

Lay Off. To cease to employ a worker.

Layout Work. The ability to read blueprints and specifications and layout and direct work for others to follow.

Machining. Turning, shaping, planing, milling, or otherwise reducing or finishing a product using machine-operated tools.

Manual Skills. Those skills performed by hand, which require or use physical skills and energy.

Masonry. The art or occupation of a mason, i.e., bricklaying, stonework, building with concrete blocks, cinder blocks, and so on.

Masonry Nailing. Driving nails into concrete blocks, bricks, and similar building materials.

Millwork. Finished carpentry work or work completed in a woodworking mill, such as assembled windows and window frames, doors and door frames.

Millwright. A subdivision of the carpentry craft; a worker who installs machinery and related components, such as conveyor systems, in mills, industrial complexes, and power plants.

Modular. Constructed with standardized units or dimensions for easy assembly and a variety of uses.

On-the-Job Training. Training for higher skills while employed in a particular craft or occupation; one is paid wages or a salary while one learns.

Partition. Something that divides; in construction, usually an interior wall separating rooms.

Pile. A long, slender shaft, usually of wood, steel, or reinforced concrete, that is driven into the ground to bear weight.

Pile Driver.   A machine for driving down piles with a pile hammer or a steam or air hammer; also, the operator of a pile driver.

Pitch.   The degree of slope of a rafter, roof, or other component of a framework.

Planer.   A machine for smoothing or shaping a wood surface.

Planing Mill.   An array of planers used for giving a smooth or decorated surface to wood.

Power Tool.   Any tool operated by motor power, usually electric.

Pre-apprenticeship.   Special training now being offered to prepare young persons to qualify for apprenticeship.

Prefabricate.   To make parts in a factory so that construction consists of assembling at the erection site.

Premium Pay.   "Top pay," or pay above what is usually expected.

Pro Rata.   Proportionately, according to some exactly figured factor.

Rafter.   Any of the parallel beams that support a roof.

Reinforced Concrete.   Concrete in which steel or other materials are used to reinforce its strength.

Resilient.   In construction, the term is applied to various types of floor covers that are somewhat elastic in application and installation, as with vinyl tiles.

Rough Framing.   The skeleton of a structure, usually built with lumber of standard dimensions. Also applies to the work involved in erecting such a structure.

Router.   A machine with a revolving vertical spindle and cutter for milling out the surface of wood or metal.

Sander.   A machine that sands surfaces to smooth, clean, or roughen them in preparation for finishing.

Scab.   One who accepts employment or replaces a union worker during a strike; one who works for less than union wages or on nonunion terms.

Scaffolding.   An array of temporary or movable platforms for workers to stand or sit on while working at a height above the floor or ground.

Scribe.   To mark a line by cutting or scratching with a pointed instrument.

Seam.   A line, groove, or ridge formed by the abutment of edges.

Seasonality.   The effect of weather and temperature on working conditions.

Sheathing.   The first covering of boards or waterproofing material on the outside wall of a frame house or on a timber roof.

Shop Course.   A course of study and training in which the student actually uses tools of the trade or craft.

Shoring.   The act of supporting with props or retaining walls; also, the system of props and braces that act as supports or shores for concrete formwork.

Siding.   Material that forms the exposed surface of outside walls of frame buildings. It is nailed over the sheathing.

Skeleton Frame.   The basic framework of main support timbers in a structure.

Sound Insulation.   Insulation designed to trap and/or direct sound waves for acoustical control.

Spline.   A thin piece of corrugated metal or a wooden strip used in construction to strengthen wood joints. It is driven into the two pieces of wood at the joint.

Stage.   A scaffold or platform for workers, usually one that can be raised or lowered by ropes and pulleys.

Stake Out.   To mark on the ground or other surface the limits and main points of the foundation of a structure before its erection. This is usually done by driving stakes into the ground.

Standard.   Something set up and established by authority, custom, or general consent as a model or example.

Stiffener.   Anything added to a material to give it more stability and strength.

Stock.   Raw material from which something is produced.

Stoppage.   In industry, this refers to a work stoppage, usually brought on by a strike or "walkout" by employees or a lockout by the employer.

Structural Steel.   Steel used in producing a metal framework for a building or other structure.

Stud.   One of the smaller uprights in the framing of the walls of a building to which sheathing, paneling, or laths are fastened.

Subcontractor.   A company or individual who enters into an agreement with a general contractor. The subcontractor usually agrees to do certain skilled work on a building. Plumbing, heating, and electrical work are subcontracted to companies that specialize in one kind of work.

Subflooring.   The basic lumber or panels laid over joists before flooring is applied.

Superintendent.   A supervisor on a construction job who directs the foremen and their work crews.

Tee.   A wood or metal joint with an abutting piece set at right angles as in a capital T.

Thermal Insulation.   Material used in building construction for protection from heat or cold.

Tolerance.   The allowable deviation from a standard; the range of variation permitted in maintaining a specified dimension in materials or in construction.

Transit.   An optical device used in land surveying and staking out foundations for construction.

Trim.   The final, finished woodwork of a structure. The term is also used in reference to painting and decorating.

Veneer.   A thin sheet of wood or other material, sometimes used as the facing on cabinets and other wood installations or assembled in sheets to form plywood.

Wage Rate.   The rate, established by contract or custom, that is used as the standard of pay for work done.

Wage Scale.   The listing of wages, highest to lowest, that shows comparative pay for particular job classifications.

Wood Turner.   One whose occupation is shaping wood by means of a lathe.

APPENDIX B

RELATED PUBLICATIONS

BROCHURES AND BOOKLETS

Listed below are brochures and booklets that you may obtain free or at a low price from various organizations interested in career development in the carpentry craft and the building and construction trades:

The "You Can Become" Series, a group of free leaflets that describe what work is performed by specific types of carpenters, what training is necessary, and what to expect when you begin work. Job titles in the series include: carpenter, residential carpenter, interior systems carpenter, cabinetmaker or millworker, floorlayer, millwright, pile driver, lather, and tile, marble, terrazzo, and dimensional stone installer. You can order one or more of these leaflets from: Apprenticeship and Training Department, United Brotherhood of Carpenters and Joiners of America, 101 Constitution Avenue NW, Washington, DC 20001.

Skills Canada, A Folder of Activities, is a collection of leaflets for training leaders wishing to develop pilot projects for craft training in the secondary schools of the Canadian provinces. To obtain this material, write: Development Officer, Skills Canada, 80 Bradford Street, Unit 23G, Barrie, Ontario, Canada L4N 6S7.

Opportunities in Building Construction Trades, by M. Sumichrast, VGM Career Horizons, NTC/Contemporary Publishing Group, 4255 West Touhy, Lincolnwood, Illinois 60646–1975.

Apprenticeship in the Building and Construction Trades, a 6-page leaflet available free from the U.S. Department of Labor Employment and Training Administration. It explains the apprenticeship training program and lists regional offices where you can obtain more information. To obtain this leaflet, contact your nearest Department of Labor regional office (see Appendix D).

National Apprenticeship Program, a 24-page booklet that explains the national system whereby construction management, labor, and government maintain standards for training carpenters and other construction tradespersons. It lists 76 apprenticable occupations and describes the U.S. Department of Labor's role in the program. This booklet is of value to training leaders. Copies can be obtained from the Federal Bureau of Apprenticeship regional offices (see Appendix D).

Apprenticeship: Past and Present, a 32-page booklet, free from the U.S. Department's Bureau of Apprenticeship and Training regional offices, describes the long history of apprenticeship in North America and how a person becomes "indentured" as an apprentice. Free from a BAT regional office (see Appendix D).

Occupational Outlook Handbook (section on Carpenters, Millwrights, Cabinetmakers), a large compendium on all classified occupations in the United States. Compiled by the Bureau of Labor Statistics, U.S. Department of Labor; issued by the Government Printing Office in Washington, DC. Also available from, NTC/Contemporary Publishing Group, 4255 West Touhy Avenue, Lincolnwood, IL 60646-1975. (Local public libraries or field offices of the U.S. Department of Labor and U.S. Employment Service usually have copies.)

Occupational Briefs No. 23—Carpenters, a 4-page summary of the trade issued by Science Research Associates, Incorporated, 155 North Wacker, Chicago, Illinois 60606.

Handbook of Trade and Technical Careers and Training, a booklet that can be obtained free of charge from the Career College Association, 750 First Street NE, Washington, DC 20002. Lists information of hundreds of careers and tells where training may be obtained.

Training Opportunities in the Job Corps, A Directory of Job Corps Centers and Programs, free from: U.S. Department of Labor, Employment and Training Administration, Washington, DC 20213.

Job Corps, Direct Referral for Affirmative Action, a 4-page leaflet, free, from: United Brotherhood of Carpenters and Joiners of America, 101 Constitution Avenue NW, Washington, DC 20001.

Career Discovery Encyclopedia, Volume 1, an occupational brief available from: Ferguson Publishing Co., 200 West Madison, Chicago, IL 60606.

Career Information Center, 6th Edition, Volume 4, available from: Macmillan Library Reference U.S.A., Prentice Hall International, Inc., 200 Old Tappan Road, Old Tappan, NJ, 07675.

PERIODICALS

The Carpenter, official publication of the United Brotherhood of Carpenters and Joiners of America, 101 Constitution Avenue NW, Washington, DC 20001. Sample copy on request.

The Constructor, Associated General Contractors of America, 1957 E Street NW, Washington, DC 20006.

The NAHB Journal of Home Building, National Association of Home Builders of the United States, Fifteenth and M Streets NW, Washington, DC 20005.

Engineering News Record, McGraw-Hill, Incorporated, 330 West Forty-second Street, New York, NY 10036. A periodical that reports on activities throughout the building and construction trades.

STATE AND TERRITORIAL APPRENTICESHIP COUNCILS/ AGENCIES

All agencies listed below, with the exception of those in Kansas and Rhode Island, operate under apprenticeship and/or training laws enacted by each state legislature. Agencies in Kansas and Rhode Island function under executive order of the governor.

Arizona

Apprenticeship Services
    Arizona Department of Economic Security
    438 West Adams Street
    Phoenix, AZ 85003

California

Division of Apprenticeship Standards
    45 Freemont Street, Suite 1040
    San Francisco, CA 94105

Connecticut

Office of Job Training and Skill Development
    Connecticut Labor Development
    200 Folly Brook Boulevard
    Wethersfield, CT 06109-1114

Delaware

Apprenticeship and Training Section
  Division of Employment & Training
  Delaware Department of Labor
  4425 North Market Street
  Station 313
  P.O. Box 9828
  Wilmington, DE 19809

District of Columbia

DC Apprenticeship Council
  500 C Street NW, Suite 241
  Washington, DC 20001

Florida

Bureau of Apprenticeship
  Division of Labor, Employment, & Training
  Department of Labor & Employment Security
  1320 Executive Center Drive, Atkins Building
  Tallahassee, FL 32399-0667

Guam

Apprenticeship Training Division
  Guam Community College
  P.O. Box 23069, GMF
  Guam, M.L. 96921

Hawaii

Apprenticeship Division
  Department of Labor and Industrial Relations
  830 Punch Bowl Street, Room 329
  Honolulu, HI 96813

Kansas

Kansas State Apprenticeship Council
  Department of Human Resources
  401 SW Topeka Boulevard
  Topeka, KS 66603-3182

Kentucky

Apprenticeship and Training
  Kentucky Labor Cabinet
  1047 U.S. 127 South, Suite 4
  Frankfort, KY 40601

Louisiana

Louisiana Department of Labor
  1001 North Twenty-third Street
  P.O. Box 94094
  Baton Rouge, LA 70804-9094

Maine

Bureau of Labor Standards
  State House Station #55
  Augusta, ME 04333

Maryland

Apprenticeship & Training Council
  1100 North Eutaw Street
  Room 606
  Baltimore, MD 21201

Massachusetts

Department of Labor and Industries
  Division of Apprentice Training
  Leverett Saltonstall Building
  100 Cambridge Street, Room 1107
  Boston, MA 02202

Minnesota

Division of Apprenticeship
  Department of Labor and Industry
  Space Center Building, 4th Floor
  443 Lafayette Road
  St. Paul, MN 55101

Montana

Apprenticeship & Training
  Bureau of Employment
  Policy Division
  Department of Labor & Industry
  715 Front Street
  Helena, MT 59601

Nevada

Nevada State Apprenticeship Council
  555 East Washington Avenue, Suite 4100
  Las Vegas, Nevada 89101

New Hampshire

New Hampshire Apprenticeship Council
  State Office Park South
  95 Pleasant Street
  Concord, NH 03301-3593

New Mexico

Apprenticeship Bureau
  Labor and Industrial Division
  New Mexico Department of Labor
  501 Mountain Road, NE
  Albuquerque, NM 87102

New York

NYS Department of Labor
  State Office Campus
  Building #12–Room 200
  Albany, NY 12240

North Carolina

Apprenticeship Division
  North Carolina Department of Labor
  4 West Edenton Street
  Raleigh, NC 27601

Ohio

Ohio State Apprenticeship Council
   145 South Front Street
   Columbus, Ohio 43215

Oregon

Apprenticeship & Training Division
   Oregon State Bureau of Labor and Industries
   800 NE Oregon Street, Room 32
   Portland, OR 97232

Pennsylvania

Apprenticeship and Training
   1301 Labor & Industry Building
   Seventh and Forster Street
   Harrisburg, PA 17120

Puerto Rico

Employment Training and Services Right to Employment Administration
   P.O. Box 364452
   San Juan, PR 00936-4452

Rhode Island

RI State Apprenticeship Shore Council
   610 Manton Avenue
   Providence, RI 02909

Vermont

Apprenticeship and Training
   Department of Labor & Industry
   5 Green Mountain Drive
   P.O. Box 488
   Montpelier, VT 05601-0488

Virgin Islands

Division of Apprenticeship & Training
   Department of Labor
   2162 King Cross Street
   P.O. Box 890, Christiansted
   St. Croix, U.S. Virgin Islands 00820-4958

Virginia

Apprenticeship and Training
  Division of Labor & Industry
  13 South Thirteenth Street
  Richmond, VA 23219

Washington

Department of Labor and Industries, ESAC Division
  General Administration Building
  MS HC-730
  46 Legion Way, SE
  Olympia, WA 98504-4530

Wisconsin

Department of Industry, Labor and Human Relations
  Employment and Training Policy Division
  P.O. Box 7972
  7201 East Washington Avenue, Room 211
  Madison, WI 53707

For information about apprenticeships in carpentry, millcabinet work, millwright work, and other building and construction trades, write: U.S. Department of Labor Employment and Training Administration, Bureau of Apprenticeship and Training, Washington, DC 20213.

APPENDIX D

REGIONAL OFFICES, U.S. BUREAU OF APPRENTICESHIP AND TRAINING

There are ten regional offices of the U.S. Bureau of Apprenticeship and Training, which are maintained by the federal government to serve the fifty states and the territorial offices (Puerto Rico, Guam, and the Virgin Islands). They are listed below beside the particular states and territories they serve. Appendix E lists the various state offices and their addresses.

Location

States Served

Regional Director
  Region I
  JFK Federal Building
  Room E-370
  Boston, MA 02203

Connecticut
Maine
Massachusetts
New Hampshire
Rhode Island
Vermont

Regional Director
  Region II
  Room 602—Federal
    Building
  201 Varick Street
  New York, NY 10014

New Jersey
New York
Puerto Rico
Virgin Islands

Location	States Served

Regional Director
  Region III
  Room 13240—Gateway
    Building
  3535 Market Street
  Philadelphia, PA 19104
	Delaware
	Maryland
	Pennsylvania
	Virginia
	West Virginia

Regional Director
  Region IV
  Room 6T71
  61 Forsyth Street SW
  Atlanta, GA 30303
	Alabama
	Florida
	Georgia
	Kentucky
	Mississippi
	North Carolina
	South Carolina
	Tennessee

Regional Director
  Region V
  6th Floor
  230 South Dearborn Street
  Chicago, IL 60604
	Illinois
	Indiana
	Michigan
	Minnesota
	Ohio
	Wisconsin

Regional Director
  Region VI
  Room 311—Federal
    Building
  525 Griffin Street
  Dallas, TX 75202
	Arkansas
	Louisiana
	New Mexico
	Oklahoma
	Texas

Regional Director
  Region VII
  Suite 1040
  1100 Main Street
  Kansas City, MO 64105-2112
	Iowa
	Kansas
	Missouri
	Nebraska

Location	**States Served**
Regional Director Region VIII Room 465 U.S. Custom House 721—Nineteenth Street Denver, CO 80202	Colorado Montana North Dakota South Dakota Utah Wyoming
Regional Director Region IX Federal Building Room 815 71 Stevenson Street San Francisco, CA 94105	Arizona California Hawaii Nevada
Regional Director Region X 1111 Third Avenue Room 925 Seattle, WA 98101-3212	Alaska Idaho Oregon Washington

STATE OFFICES, U.S. BUREAU OF APPRENTICESHIP AND TRAINING

U.S. Bureau of Apprenticeship and Training (USDL-BAT) maintains an office in each of the fifty U.S. states, as listed here. A person seeking to enroll for training in a particular state can contact his or her state office for information on how to do so.

Alabama

State Director
  USDL-BAT
  Medical Forum Building, Room 648
  950 Twenty-second Street North
  Birmingham, AL 35203

Alaska

State Director
  USDL-BAT
  Calais Building
  3301 C Street, Suite 201
  Anchorage, AK 99503

Arizona

State Director
  USDL-BAT
  Suite 302
  3221 North Sixteenth Street
  Phoenix, AZ 85016

Arkansas

State Director
 USDL-BAT
 Room 3507–Federal Building
 700 West Capitol Street
 Little Rock, AR 72201

California

State Director
 USDL-BAT
 1301 Clay Street
 Oakland, CA 94612-5217

Colorado

State Director
 USDL-BAT
 Room 469–U.S. Custom House
 721 Nineteenth Street
 Denver, CO 80202

Connecticut

State Director
 USDL-BAT
 Room 367–Federal Building
 135 High Street
 Hartford, CT 06103

Delaware

State Director
 USDL-BAT
 Lock Box 36–Federal Building
 844 King Street
 Wilmington, DE 19801

Florida

State Director
 USDL-BAT
 Suite 4140–City Centre Building
 227 North Bronough Street
 Tallahassee, FL 32301

Georgia

State Director
  USDL-BAT
  6 Room 6T80
  61 Forsyth Street SW
  Atlanta, GA 30303

Hawaii

State Director
  USDL-BAT
  Room 5-117
  300 Ala Moana Boulevard
  Honolulu, HI 96850

Idaho

State Director
  USDL-BAT
  Suite 204
  1115 North Curtes
  Boise, ID 83706-1234

Illinois

State Director
  USDL-BAT
  Room 708
  230 South Dearborn Street
  Chicago, IL 60604

Indiana

State Director
  USDL-BAT
  Room 414, Federal Building/U.S. Courthouse
  46 East Ohio Street
  Indianapolis, IN 46204

Iowa

State Director
  USDL-BAT
  Room 715–A Federal Building
  210 Walnut Street
  Des Moines, IA 50309

Kansas

State Director
USDL-BAT
Room 247–Federal Building
444 SE Quincy Street
Topeka, KS 66683-3571

Kentucky

State Director
USDL-BAT
Room 187-J–Federal Building
600 Martin Luther King Place
Louisville, KY 40202

Louisiana

State Director
USDL-BAT
Suite 1043
501 Magazine Street
New Orleans, LA 70130

Maine

State Director
USDL-BAT
Room 401–Federal Building
68 Sewell Street
Augusta, ME 04330

Maryland

State Director
USDL-BAT
300 West Pratt Street, Room 200
Baltimore, MD 21201

Massachusetts

State Director
USDL-BAT
Room E-370–JFK Federal Building
Government Center
Boston, MA 02203

Michigan

State Director
  USDL-BAT
  Room 304
  801 South Waverly
  Lansing, MI 48917

Minnesota

State Director
  USDL-BAT
  Room 134–Federal Building/U.S. Courthouse
  316 Robert Street
  St. Paul, MN 55101

Mississippi

State Director
  USDL-BAT
  Suite 410–Federal Building
  100 West Capital Street
  Jackson, MS 39269

Missouri

State Director
  USDL-BAT
  Room 9.102E
  Robert A. Young Federal Building
  1222 Spruce Street
  St. Louis, MO 63103

Montana

State Director
  USDL-BAT
  Room 396–Drawer #10055
  Federal Office Building
  301 South Park Avenue
  Helena, MT 59626-0055

Nebraska

State Director
USDL-BAT
Room 801
106 South Fifteenth Street
Omaha, NE 68102

Nevada

State Director
USDL-BAT
Room 311—P.O. Building
301 Stewart Avenue
Las Vegas, NV 89101

New Hampshire

State Director
USDL-BAT
143 North Main Street, Room 205
Concord, NH 03301

New Jersey

State Director
USDL-BAT
Parkway Towers
Building E, 3rd Floor
485-Route #1 South
Iselin, NJ 08830

New Mexico

State Director
USDL-BAT
505 Marquette, Room 830
Albuquerque, NM 87102

New York

State Director
USDL-BAT
Room 809–Federal Building
North Pearl & Clinton Avenue
Albany, NY 12207

North Carolina

State Director
  USDL-BAT
  Somerset Park, Suite 205
  4407 Bland Road
  Raleigh, NC 27609

North Dakota

State Director
  USDL-BAT
  Room 332
  304 East Broadway
  Bismarck, ND 58501

Ohio

State Director
  USDL-BAT
  Room 605
  200 North High Street
  Columbus, OH 43215

Oklahoma

State Director
  USDL-BAT
  1500 South Midwest Boulevard
  Suite 202
  Midwest City, OK 73110

Oregon

State Director
  USDL-BAT
  629 Federal Building
  1220 SW Third Avenue
  Portland, OR 97204

Pennsylvania

State Director
  USDL-BAT
  Room 773–Federal Building
  228 Walnut Street
  Harrisburg, PA 17108

126 Opportunities in Carpentry Careers

Rhode Island

State Director
USDL-BAT
100 Hartford Avenue
Providence, RI 02909

South Carolina

State Director
USDL-BAT
Room 838–South Thurmond Federal Building
1835 Assembly Street
Columbia, SC 29201

South Dakota

State Director
USDL-BAT
Oxbow 1 Building
Room 204
2400 West Forty-ninth Street
Sioux Falls, SD 57105

Tennessee

State Director
USDL-BAT
Airport Executive Plaza
1321 Murfreesboro Road
Suite 541
Nashville, TN 37210

Texas

State Director
USDL-BAT
Room 2102–VA Building
2320 LaBranch Street
Houston, TX 77004

Utah

State Director
  USDL-BAT
  Suite 101
  1600 West 2200 South
  Salt Lake City, UT 84119

Vermont

State Director
  USDL-BAT
  Federal Building
  11 Elmwood Avenue, Room 612
  Burlington, Vermont 05401

Virginia

State Director
  USDL-BAT
  700 Centre, Suite 546
  704 East Franklin Street
  Richmond, VA 23219

Washington

State Director
  USDL-BAT
  Suite 100
  1400 Talbot Road South
  Renton, WA 98055

West Virginia

State Director
  USDL-BAT
  Suite 203
  1108 Third Avenue
  Huntington, WV 25301

Wisconsin

State Director
  USDL-BAT
  Room 303-Federal Center
  212 East Washington Avenue
  Madison, WI 53703

Wyoming

State Director
  USDL-BAT
  American National Bank Building
  1912 Capitol Avenue, Room 508
  Cheyenne, WY 82001-3661

ACCREDITED TRADE SCHOOLS

In addition to the apprenticeship training programs recognized and approved by the federal government, industry, and the union, there are a number of private trade and technical schools that teach carpentry skills and are accredited by the National Association of Trade and Technical Schools. The names and addresses of these schools include:

AMERICAN SCHOOLS

Alabama

Atmore State Technical College
P.O. Box 1119
Atmore, AL 36504

Chauncey Sparks State Technical College
P.O. Drawer 580
Eufaula, AL 36027

Douglas MacArthur Technical College
P.O. Box 649
Opp, AL 36467

Gadsden State Community College
P.O. Box 227
Gadsden, AL 35902-0227

George C. Wallace State Community College-Hanceville
    801 Main Street NW, P.O. Box 2000
    Hanceville, AL 35077-2000

Harry M. Ayers State Technical College
    1801 Colemen Road, P.O. Box 1647
    Anniston, AL 36202

J. F. Ingram State Technical College
    P.O. Box 209
    Deatsville, AL 36022

John C. Calhoun State Community College
    P.O. Box 2216
    Decatur, AL 35609-2216

Lawson State Community College
    3060 Wilson Road, SW
    Birmingham, AL 35221

Opelika State Technical College
    P.O. Box 2268
    Opelika, AL 36803-2268

Arizona
    Central Arizona College
    8470 North Overfield Road
    Coolidge, AZ 85228-9778

Easter Arizona College
    Church Street
    Thatcher, AZ 85552-0769

Arkansas

Black River Technical College
    Hwy. 304, P.O. Box 468
    Pocahontas, AR 72455

Crowley's Ridge Technical School
    P.O. Box 925
    Forrest City, AR 72335

Northwest Technical Institute
    P.O. Box A
    Springdale, AR 72765

Pulaski Technical College
  3000 West Scenic Drive
  North Little Rock, AR 72118

Quapaw Technical Institute
  201 Vocational-Tech Drive
  Hot Springs, AR 71913

Red River Technical College
  P.O. Box 140
  Hope, AR 71801

California

College of the Redwoods
  7351 Tompkins Hill Road
  Eureka, CA 95501-9302

El Camino College
  16007 Crenshaw Boulevard
  Torrance, CA 90506

Fresno City College
  1101 East University Avenue
  Fresno, CA 93741

Laney College
  900 Fallon Street
  Oakland, CA 94607

Los Angeles Training Technical College
  400 West Washington Boulevard
  Los Angeles, CA 90015-4181

San Joaquin Delta College
  5151 Pacific Avenue
  Stockton, CA 95207

Sierra College
  5000 Rocklin Road
  Rocklin, CA 95677

Florida

Manatee Vocational-Technical Center
  5603 Thirty-fourth Street, W
  Bradenton, FL 34210

Miami Lakes Technical Education Center
    5780 Northwest 158th Street
    Miami Lakes, FL 33169

Pinellas Technical Education Center-Clearwater Campus
    6100 154th Avenue N
    Clearwater, FL 34620

Saint Augustine Technical Center
    2980 Collins Avenue
    Saint Augustine, FL 32095

Washington-Holmes Area Vocational-Technical Center
    209 Hoy Street
    Chipley, FL 32428

Georgia

Atlanta Area Technical School
    1560 Stewart Avenue, SW
    Atlanta, GA 30310

Columbus Technical Institute
    928 Forty-fifth Street
    Columbus, GA 31904-6572

Griffin Technical Institute
    501 Varsity Road
    Griffin, GA 30223

Gwinnett Technical Institute
    1250 Atkinson Road, P.O. Box 1505
    Lawrenceville, GA 30246-1505

Lanier Technical Institute
    P.O. Box 58
    Oakwood, GA 30566

North Georgia Technical Institute
    Georgia Hwy. 197, P.O. Box 65
    Clarkesville, GA 30523

Pickens Technical Institute
    100 Pickens Tech Drive
    Jasper, GA 30143

Hawaii

Hawaii Community College
200 West Kawili Street
Hilo, HI 96720-4091

Honolulu Community College
874 Dillingham Boulevard
Honolulu, HI 96817

Idaho

College of Southern Idaho
P.O. Box 1238
Twin Falls, ID 83301

North Idaho College
1000 West Garden Avenue
Coeur D'Alene, ID 83814

Illinois

Black Hawk College-Quad Cities
6600 Thirty-fourth Avenue
Moline, IL 61265

Washburne Trade School
3233 West Thirty-first Street
Chicago, IL 60623

Iowa

Des Moines Community College
2006 Ankeny Boulevard
Ankeny, IA 50021

Indian Hills Community College
525 Grandview
Ottumwa, IA 52501

Iowa Central Community College
330 Avenue M
Fort Dodge, IA 50501

Iowa Valley Community College
P.O. Box 536
Marshalltown, IA 50158

Northeast Iowa Community College
  Hwy. 150 S, P.O. Box 400
  Calmar, IA 52132-0400

Southwestern Community College
  1501 Townline
  Creston, IA 50801

Western Iowa Technical Community College
  4647 Stone Avenue, P.O. Box 265
  Sioux City, IA 51102-0265

Kansas

Hutchinson Community College
  1300 North Plum Street
  Hutchinson, KS 67501

Johnson County Area Vocational-Technical School
  311 East Park
  Olathe, KS 66061

Kansas City Area Vocational Technical School
  2220 North Fifty-ninth Street
  Kansas City, KS 66104

Kaw Area Vocational-Technical School
  5724 Huntoon
  Topeka, KS 66604

Liberal Area Vocational Technical School
  P.O. Box 1599
  Liberal, KS 67905-1599

Manhattan Area Technical Center
  3136 Dickens Avenue
  Manhattan, KS 66502

North Central Kansas Area Vocational Technical School
  Hwy. 24, P.O. Box 507
  Beloit, KS 67420

Northeast Kansas Area Vocational Technical School
  1501 West Riley Street, P.O. Box 277
  Atchison, KS 66002

Northwest Kansas Area Vocational Technical School
    P.O. Box 668
    Goodland, KS 67735

Salina Area Vocational Technical School
    2562 Scanlan Avenue
    Salina, KS 67401

Southeast Kansas Area Vocational Technical School
    Sixth and Roosevelt
    Coffeyville, KS 67337

Wichita Area Vocational Technical School
    428 South Broadway
    Wichita, KS 67202-3910

Kentucky

Ashland State Vocational Technical School
    4818 Roberts Drive
    Ashland, KY 41102

Kentucky Technical-Madisonville State Vocational Technical School
    150 School Avenue
    Madisonville, KY 42431

Mayo State Vocational Technical School
    Third Street
    Paintsville, KY 41240

Northern Kentucky State Vocational-Technical School
    1025 Amsterdam Road
    Covington, KY 41011

Louisiana

Alexandria Regional Technical Institute
    4311 South MacArthur Drive
    Alexandria, LA 71302-3137

Junionville Memorial Technical Institute
    P.O. Box 725
    New Roads, LA 70760

Sullivan Technical Institute
    1710 Sullivan Drive
    Bogalusa, LA 70427

West Jefferson Technical Institute
475 Manhattan Boulevard
Harvey, LA 70058

Maine

Eastern Maine Technical College
354 Hogan Road
Bangor, ME 04401

Landing School of Boat Building and Design
P.O. Box 1490
Kennebunkport, ME 04046

Northern Maine Technical College
33 Edgemont Drive
Presque Isle, ME 04769

Southern Maine Technical College
Fort Road
South Portland, ME 04106

Washington County Technical College
RR 1, P.O. Box 22C
Calais, ME 04619

Maryland

Howard Community College
Little Patuxent Parkway
Columbia, MD 21044

Massachusetts

North Bennet Street School
39 North Bennet Street
Boston, MA 02113

Michigan

Bay De Noc Community College
2001 North Lincoln Road
Escanaba, MI 49289

Macomb Community College
    14500 Twelve Mile Road
    Warren, MI 48093-3896

Northern Michigan University
    1401 Presque Isle
    Marquette, MI 49855

Minnesota

Alexandria Technical College
    1601 Jefferson Street
    Alexandria, MN 56308

Hennepin Technical College
    1820 North Xenium Lane
    Plymouth, MN 55441

Hutchinson-Willmar Technical College-Willmar Campus
    P.O. Box 1097
    Willmar, MN 56201

Minneapolis Technical College
    1415 Hennepin Avenue
    Minneapolis, MN 55403

Minnesota Riverland Technical College-Austin Campus
    1900 Eighth Avenue, NW
    Austin, MN 55912

Minnesota Riverland Technical College-Faribault Campus
    1225 Southwest Third Street
    Faribault, MN 55021

Minnesota Riverland Technical College-Rochester Campus
    1926 College View Road, SE
    Rochester, MN 55904

Northwest Technical College-Detroit Lakes
    900 Hwy. 34 E
    Detroit Lakes, MN 56501

Northwest Technical College-East Grand Forks
    Hwy. 220 N
    East Grand Forks, MN 56721

Northwest Technical College-Moorhead
    1900 Twenty-eighth Avenue S.
    Moorhead, MN 56560

Red Wing-Winona Technical College-Red Wing Campus
    Hwy. 58 at Pioneer Road
    Red Wing, MN 55066

Saint Cloud Technical College
    1540 Northway Drive
    Saint Cloud, MN 56303

Southwestern Technical College-Jackson Campus
    401 West Street
    Jackson, MN 56143

Southwestern Technical College-Pipestone Campus
    P.O. Box 250
    Pipestone, MN 56164

Saint Paul Technical College
    235 Marshall Avenue
    Saint Paul, MN 55102

Mississippi

East Central Community College
    Decatur, MS 39327

Hinds Community College-Raymond Campus
    Raymond, MS 39154

Missouri

Macon Area Vocational School
    Hwy. 63 N
    Macon, MO 63552

Ranken Technical College
    4431 Finney Avenue
    Saint Louis, MO 63113

Rolla Area Vocational-Technical School
    1304 East Tenth Street
    Rolla, MO 65401

Waynesville Area Vocational School
810 Roosevelt
Waynesville, MO 65583

Montana

Helena Vocational-Technical Center
1115 North Roberts Street
Helena, MT 59601

Nebraska

Mid Plains Community College
416 North Jeffers
North Platte, NE 69101

New Hampshire

New Hampshire Technical College at Manchester
1066 Front Street
Manchester, NH 03102

New Mexico

Albuquerque Technical-Vocational Institute
525 Buena Vista, SE
Albuquerque, NM 87106

Crownpoint Institute of Technology
P.O. Box 849
Crownpoint, NM 87313

New York

Mohawk Valley Community College
1101 Sherman Drive
Utica, NY 13501

SUNY College of Technology at Delhi
Delhi, NY 13753

North Carolina

Alamance Community College
P.O. Box 8000
Graham, NC 27253

Cleveland Community College
    137 South Post Road
    Shelby, NC 28150

Rockingham Community College
    P.O. Box 38
    Wenthworth, NC 27375-0038

Vance-Granville Community College
    State Road 1126, P.O. Box 917
    Henderson, NC 27536

North Dakota

United Tribes Technical College
    3315 University Drive
    Bismark, ND 58501

Ohio

Eastland Career Center
    4465 South Hamilton Road
    Groveport, OH 43125

Tri-County Vocational School
    15675 SR 691
    Nelsonville, OH 45764

Oklahoma

Central Oklahoma Area Vocational Technical School
    Three Court Circle
    Drumright, OK 74030

Great Plains Area Vocational-Technical School
    4500 West Lee Boulevard
    Lawton, OK 73505

Kiamichi AVTS SD #7-Talihina Campus
    Rte. 2 & Hwy. 63A, P.O. Box 1800
    Talihina, OK 74571

Metro Tech Vocational Technical Center
    1900 Springlake Drive
    Oklahoma City, OK 73111

Southern Oklahoma Area Vocational-Technical Center
2610 Sam Noble Pkwy.
Ardmore, OK 73401

Pennsylvania

Bucks County Community College
Swamp Road
Newtown, PA 18940

Community College of Allegheny County
800 Allegheny Avenue
Pittsburgh, PA 15233-1895

Pennsylvania College of Technology
One College Avenue
Williamsport, PA 17701

Thaddeus Stevens State School of Technology
750 East King Street
Lancaster, PA 17602

Triangle Technical-Dubois
P.O. Box 551
Dubois, PA 15801

Rhode Island

New England Institute of Technology
2500 Post Road
Warwick, RI 02886

South Carolina

Bob Jones University
Greenville, SC 29614

Greenville Technical College
Station B, P.O. Box 5616
Greenville, SC 29606-5616

South Dakota

Lake Area Vocational Technical Institute
230 Eleventh Street NE
Watertown, SD 57201

Texas

Texas State Technical College-Harlingen Campus
2424 Boxwood
Harlingen, TX 78550-3697

Utah

Ogden-Weber Applied Technology Center
559 East AVC Lane
Ogden, UT 84404-6704

Salt Lake Community College
P.O. Box 30808
Salt Lake City, UT 84130

Utah Valley Community College
800 West 1200 S
Orem, UT 84058

Washington

Bates Technical College
1101 South Yakima Avenue
Tacoma, WA 98405

Northwest School of Wooden Boatbuilding
251 Otto Street
Port Townsend, WA 98368

Olympic College
1600 Chester Avenue
Bremerton, WA 98310-1699

Seattle Central Community College
1701 Broadway
Seattle, WA 98122

Seattle Vocational Institute
315 Twenty-second Avenue S
Seattle, WA 98144

West Virginia

Raleigh County Vocational-Technical Center
410-1/2 Stanaford Road
Beckley, WV 25801

Wisconsin

Chippewa Valley Technical College
620 West Clairemont Avenue
Eau Claire, WI 54701

Gateway Technical College
3520 30th Avenue
Kenosha, WI 53144-1690

Milwaukee Area Technical College
700 West State Street
Milwaukee, WI 53233

Northeast Wisconsin Technical College
2740 West Mason Street, P.O. Box 19042
Green Bay, WI 54307-9042

Wisconsin Area Vocational Training and Adult Education System District
Number Four
3550 Anderson Street
Madison, WI 53704

Wisconsin Indianhead Technical College
505 Pine Ridge Drive, P.O. Box 10B
Shell Lake, WI 54871

Wyoming

Laramie County Community College
1400 East College Drive
Cheyenne, WY 82007

CANADIAN SCHOOLS

Alberta

Southern Alberta Institute of Technology
1301 - 16 Avenue Northwest
Calgary, Alberta
T2M 0L4

Northern Alberta Institute of Technology
    11762 - 106 Street
    Edmonton, Alberta
    T5G 2R1

British Columbia

British Columbia Institute of Technology
    3700 Willingdon Avenue
    Burnaby, BC
    V5G 3H2

Camosun College
    Landsdowne Campus 3100 Foul Bay Road
    Victoria, BC
    V8P 5J2

College of New Caledonia
    3330 Twenty-second Avenue
    Prince George, BC
    V2N 1P8

College of the Rockies
    Cranbrook Campus 2700 College Way
    P.O. Box 8500
    Cranbrook, BC
    V1C 5L7

Kwantlen University College
    12666 Seventy-second Avenue
    Surrey, BC
    V3W 2M8

Malaspina University-College
    900 Fifth Street
    Nanaimo, BC
    V9R 5S5

Northern Lights College
    11401 Eighth Street
    Dawsons Creek, BC
    V1G 4G2

Northwest Community College
5331 McConnell Avenue
Terrace, BC
V8G 4X2

Okanagan University College
KLO Campus 1000 KLO Road
Kelowna, BC
V1Y 4X8

Univeristy College of the Cariboo
900 McGill Road
Kamloops, BC
V2C 5N3

Univeristy College of the Fraser Valley
West Campus 33844 King Road
Abbotsford, BC
V2S 7M9

New Brunswick

CCNB Campbellton
C.P. 309 Rue village
Campbellton, NB
E3N 3G7

TRADE ASSOCIATIONS

There are trade associations of building trades management and trade associations of building trades workers. Here is a list of both, as they relate to carpentry and its allied trades. Many of these associations have programs to assist young people who want to enter their respective trades.

CARPENTERS

Associated General Contractors of America, Inc.
  1957 E Street, NW
  Washington, DC 20006

Home Builders Institute, National Association of Home Builders
  1201 Fifteenth Street, NW
  Washington, DC 20005

United Brotherhood of Carpenters and Joiners of America
  101 Constitution Avenue, NW
  Washington, DC 20001

Associated Builders and Contractors
  1300 North Seventeenth Street
  Rosslyn, VA 22209

CARPET INSTALLERS

Floor Covering Installation Contractors of America
    P.O. Box 948
    Dalton, GA 30722-0948

International Brotherhood of Painters and Allied Trades
    1750 New York Avenue, NW
    Washington, DC 20006

United Brotherhood of Carpenters and Joiners of America
    101 Constitution Avenue, NW
    Washington, DC 20001

DRYWALL WORKERS AND LATHERS

Associated Builders and Contractors
    1300 North Seventeenth Street
    Rosslyn, VA 22209

International Brotherhood of Painters and Allied Trades
    1750 New York Avenue, NW
    Washington, DC 20006

United Brotherhood of Carpenters and Joiners of America
    101 Constitution Avenue, NW
    Washington, DC 20001

Home Builders Institute, National Association of Home Builders
    1201 Fifteenth Street, NW
    Washington, DC 20005